POP-UP

EMBROIDERY

POP-UP
EMBROIDERY

A beginner's guide to modern raised stitches

Techniques and projects to bring new dimensions to your stitchery

ASHLEY DENN

Abrams, New York

Library of Congress Control Number: 2022948258

ISBN: 978-1-4197-6666-4

This book was conceived, designed, and produced by
Quarto Publishing, an imprint of The Quarto Group
6 Blundell Street
London N7 9BH

Senior Editor: Emma Harverson
Designer: Sally Bond
Project photography: Nicki Dowey
Step photography: Ashley Denn
Art Director: Gemma Wilson
Publisher: Lorraine Dickey

Printed and bound in China

10 9 8 7 6 5 4 3 2 1

Abrams books are available at special discounts when purchased
in quantity for premiums and promotions as well as fundraising
or educational use. Special editions can also be created to
specification. For details, contact specialsales@abramsbooks.com
or the address below.

ABRAMS The Art of Books
195 Broadway, New York, NY 10007
abramsbooks.com

MIX
Paper | Supporting
responsible forestry
FSC® C008047

CONTENTS

MEET ASHLEY

I grew up in a family with two wonderfully creative parents. As a kid, my dad's hobbies included guitar playing and carpentry; my mom had a love of crafting and sewed all of my outfits for holidays and school pictures. When I was very young, my mom would punch holes into different-shaped pieces of cardboard and give me yarn so I could sew alongside her. As I grew, she taught me how to create simple cross stitch and embroidery pieces. In 2018, I picked up a needle and thread for the first time in my adult life. All those childhood memories came flooding back, filling me with such elation that I haven't stopped stitching since. The joy of completing a handmade project is what I hope to share with you.

This book is broken into two parts: the stitches and the projects. The first part provides step-by-step guides for completing thirty hand-embroidery stitches and techniques. There are five flat stitches that are used to fill in the spaces between the raised embroidery elements. I have also included twenty raised stitches that add texture and dimension to each design. Finally, there are five raised techniques that use materials other than thread for additional dimension. This first part will be used as a reference guide as you stitch through each of the patterns.

The second part of the book includes twenty contemporary hand-embroidery projects, allowing opportunities to practice all thirty stitches you have learned. The patterns vary in both design and difficulty, and are broken down into three levels. To start, level 1 patterns use only a few raised stitches with simple designs. Level 2 adds more details, includes more raised stitches, and introduces a couple of raised techniques. Finally, level 3 patterns become a bit more complex, each using a variety of flat stitches, raised stitches, and raised techniques.

The flow of this book is intended to gradually expand your knowledge and skill within the world of raised embroidery. After learning a variety of new stitches in part one you are provided with opportunities to slowly build up your embroidery skills in part two. To develop your techniques the projects are intended to be stitched in order, but you may find yourself itching to get to a specific few first. Whichever order you choose to stitch the projects in, just remember: hand embroidery is a practice of patience. As you stitch through each pattern, remember to enjoy the moments of creating.

BEFORE YOU START

In this section, you'll look over some of the materials and tools used in embroidery. Then you'll learn the basics of setting up and closing your hoop, as well as a few tips and tricks that will help you on your stitching journey.

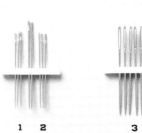

1 2   3

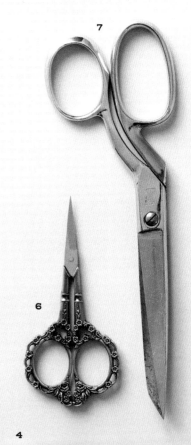

7

6

4

5

TOOLS AND MATERIALS

Every project will have its own list of supplies. This section takes a closer look at some of the tools and materials that will be used throughout the projects.

Needles

Embroidery needles (**1**) come in different sizes. When choosing a needle, a general rule to follow is the shaft of the needle should be about as thick as the thread. You should be able to pull the needle and thread through the fabric easily without a lot of resistance, making a hole large enough for the thread to pass through, but not any larger.

Crewel embroidery needles—sizes 1 to 5 (**2**)—are ideal for the projects in this book. Size 1 is perfect for a full six strands of thread. Sizes 2 to 5 work well when using fewer strands of thread.

Large eye needles (**3**) are used for working thicker, non-thread materials like yarn or string. They are also helpful when combining more than six strands of thread at a time.

Pens

Water-soluble pens (**4**) allow you to draw the design onto the fabric, and any exposed markings after stitching can be washed off with water.

Heat-sensitive erasable pens (**5**) have a finer point and use ink that disappears when heat is applied, such as from an iron or blow dryer.

Scissors

Embroidery scissors (**6**) are recommended because they have short, sharp blades that allow close and precise cutting.

Fabric scissors (**7**) allow you to cut and trim fabric, leaving behind clean edges. Scalloped or zigzagged fabric scissors help to prevent the fabric from fraying.

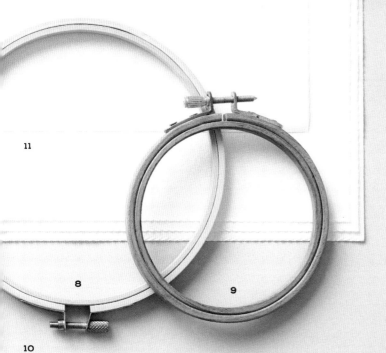

11

8

9

10

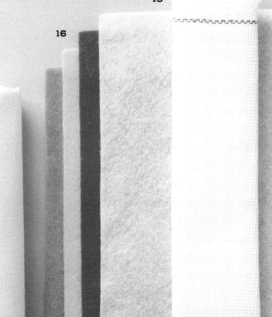

14

12

13

Stabilizer

Stick-on, water-soluble stabilizer **(11)** is a popular choice. It sticks to the front of the fabric, providing support while you stitch. You can also draw or print the design onto the stabilizer. It washes away with water and saves the fabric from being marked up.

Tear-away stabilizer is my preferred choice. I like to place it behind my fabric in the hoop to provide a more sturdy surface. You can tear away the stabilizer after stitching or leave it in the hoop with the fabric since it is not seen from the front.

Fabric

Raised embroidery requires sturdy fabrics with little stretch. Linen **(12)**, 100 percent cotton **(13)**, and canvas **(14)** are ideal fabrics for raised stitching.

Aida cloth

Often used for cross stitch work, Aida cloth **(15)** is a sturdy fabric that can be used in making embroidery slips. Any size of Aida cloth will work for the projects in this book.

Felt

Craft felt **(16)**, found in any craft aisle or store, can be layered and easily stitched through with most embroidery needles.

15

16

Wooden embroidery hoops

Wooden hoops are most commonly used in hand embroidery as they grip the fabric well. Bamboo hoops **(8)** are the most popular and the least expensive option. Beech hoops **(9)** have a nice finish, are strong, and hold the fabric well.

Thread

Six-stranded cotton thread **(10)** is used for every project. Strands can be separated (see page 11) to change the depth of the stitch. Suggested DMC thread color indicators are listed for each project, but you can choose any color.

PLACING THE FABRIC IN THE HOOP

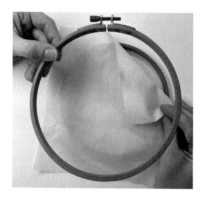

1 Iron the fabric and center it on top of the inner hoop. Then place the outer hoop over the fabric.

2 With the outer hoop over the fabric, press it gently down into place around the inner hoop. Tighten the screw to secure the fabric.

3 Gently pull the edges of the fabric evenly all the way around the hoop until it is taut. The fabric should sound like a soft drum when tapped.

THREAD WRAPPING

One of my favorite ways to finish an embroidery project is to customize the outer hoop with thread or yarn. I use bamboo hoops for thread wrapping and love how the wrapped thread adds texture and color to the piece.

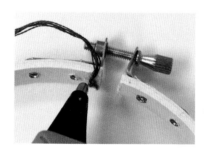

1 Leave the skein of thread uncut and leave it in the skein or on a bobbin. Glue the tip of the thread to the underside of the hoop, at one of the open edges under the screw.

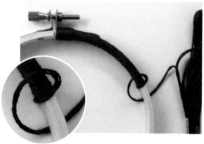

2 Tightly wrap the thread around the hoop, laying each new wrap next to the previous one without any overlaps. Continue wrapping all the way around until the hoop is covered.

3 Glue the thread to the underside of the hoop at the other open edge under the screw. Allow the glue to dry and trim any remaining thread with scissors.

CLOSING THE HOOP

1 After positioning the completed piece in the hoop where you would like it to sit in the frame, turn the hoop over. Trim the fabric to about 1 inch (2.5 cm) all the way around the hoop.

2 Using six strands of thread in any color, use the needle to weave the thread in and out of the trimmed fabric outside the hoop. End the thread right next to where it began.

3 Take the two ends of thread and pull them tight, closing the fabric over the inner hoop. Tie a knot to secure it and trim the leftover length of thread.

HELPFUL TIPS

USING GUIDELINES

SEPARATING STRANDS OF THREAD

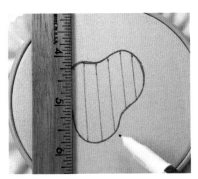

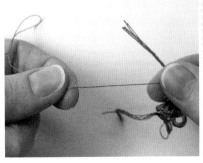

Guidelines are a great strategy to help keep your stitches straight. They are most helpful when using satin stitch or long and short stitch. Use a ruler and a water-soluble or heat-sensitive pen to draw evenly spaced guidelines across the area you want to stitch.

1 Cut the thread to around 18 inches (46 cm) in length. Separate one strand from the bunch.

2 Pinch the bunch of thread with one hand, and gently pull out the single strand with your other hand.

STARTING KNOTS

1 Using one end of the thread, create a loop and tuck the end of the thread through the loop.

2 Pull the thread through tightly, to create the knot. Repeat to secure if necessary.

ENDING KNOTS

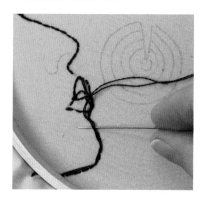 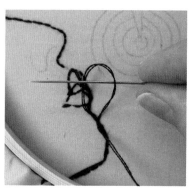 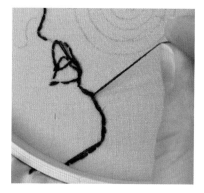

1 Turn the hoop over to the back side. Bring the needle and thread under some of the stitches.

2 Pull the thread through until there is a small loop. Then bring the needle and thread through the loop.

3 Pull tightly to secure the thread. Complete steps 1 to 3 at least one more time.

TRANSFERRING THE DESIGN TO THE FABRIC

Transferring a design from template to fabric is the first step in completing an embroidery piece. You can draw the design onto the fabric by hand, using the templates and instructions on page 132, or iron the design directly onto the fabric using the transfer sheets provided.

DRAWING-ON TRANSFERS

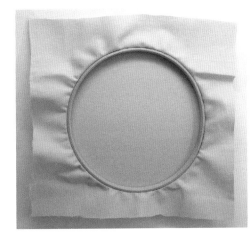

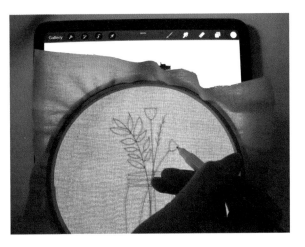

1 Iron the fabric and place it in the embroidery hoop. Turn the hoop over so the inner hoop is facing upward.

2 Place the hoop against a light source, such as a window or brightly lit screen, then place the template between the fabric and the light source. Use a water-soluble or heat-sensitive pen to trace the image onto the fabric.

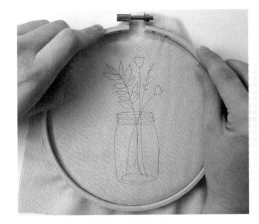

3 Remove the fabric from the hoop and replace it with the image and outer hoop facing upward. Gently pull the fabric around the entire hoop until the fabric is taut, being careful not to distort the image.

IRON-ON TRANSFERS

Pre-iron the fabric and cut it to the desired size. Trim the iron-on transfer template (located in the envelope at the back of the book) and place it where you would like the design to sit on the fabric. With high heat, iron the template to the fabric. Apply steady and even pressure to the iron, moving in small circles and being careful to ensure the template does not move. Continue pressing until the transfer image is no longer sticking to the paper. Allow the transferred design to cool for a few minutes and then gently peel the template paper from the fabric.

STITCHES & TECHNIQUES

STRAIGHT STITCH

Straight stitch is a single stitch. It is the foundation for many other embroidery stitches and can be used by itself or grouped together to create various designs.

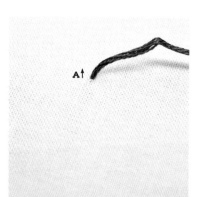

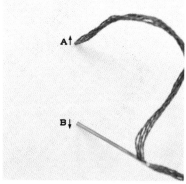

1 Bring the needle and thread to the front of the fabric, up through A.

2 Take the needle and thread to the back of the fabric, down through B.

3 Pull the thread all the way through the fabric and secure it on the back with a knot. One single straight stitch is pictured.

BACK STITCH

Back stitch is used for outlining straight and curved lines. Shorter stitches are best for curved lines while longer stitches can be used for straight lines.

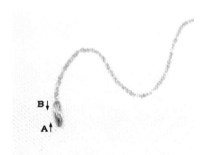

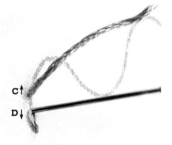

1 Start by creating one straight stitch (see page 16). Bring the needle up at A and down at B.

2 Bring the needle up at C. Keep the distance between C and B the same as between A and B.

3 Take the needle and thread back down to the back of the fabric, at D, using the same hole as B.

4 Repeat steps 2 and 3 for all remaining stitches, always working backward. To finish, secure the thread on the back with a knot.

LONG AND SHORT STITCH

Long and short stitch is great for filling in larger areas and shapes while also adding texture. When more than one color of thread is used, it provides a gradual shaded effect.

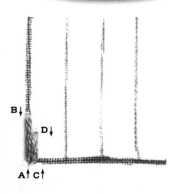

2 For the second row, and all rows except the last one, use only long stitches. Pass the needle through the holes of the previous row each time. Continue stitching rows of long stitches until the shape is almost filled in.

1 Begin the first row with a series of straight stitches, alternating in length. The short stitches should be half the length of the long stitches. Bring the needle up at A, down at B, up at C, and down at D. Continue this pattern until the row is complete.

3 Stitch the last row with a series of alternating long and short stitches. To finish, secure the thread on the back with a knot.

STEM STITCH

Stem stitch can be used for outlining straight and curved lines, and lettering, and is often used for stems of plants. It is known for its rope-like appearance.

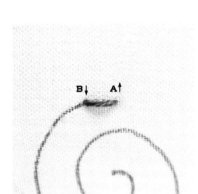

1 Start by creating one straight stitch. Bring the needle up at A and down at B.

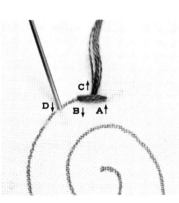

2 Bring the needle up halfway between A and B, at C. Then, keeping the length the same as the first stitch, bring the needle down at D.

3 Repeat step 2 for all remaining stitches. Make sure to keep the thread below the needle for every stitch, as shown, to maintain the pattern. To finish, secure the thread on the back with a knot.

SATIN STITCH

Satin stitch is used to fill in small- to medium-sized areas with a smooth finish. Satin stitches should be worked closely side by side, without pulling the fabric.

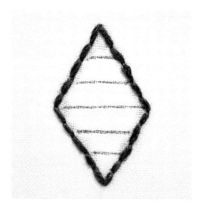

1 First, outline the shape with back stitch (pictured, see page 17) or stem stitch (see page 19). This helps to give clean edges to the finished shape.

2 Using two to three strands of thread and starting at one end of the shape, bring the needle up through the fabric, on the outside of the outline.

3 Take the needle down through the fabric, on the opposite outside edge of the outline. Repeat steps 2 and 3, to fill the area.

OVERCAST STITCH

Overcast stitch, also known as trailing, is used for producing raised outlines. Create a variety of thicknesses by increasing the number of strands, or by using yarn or macramé cord for the core.

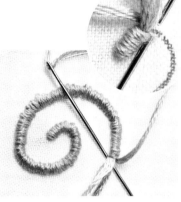

1 Start by pulling your core threads to the front of the hoop, knotting them at the back to secure.

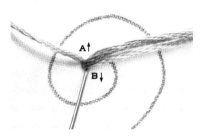

2 With the working thread (pink), bring the needle up at A, on one side of the core threads, and down at B on the other side of the core threads.

3 Guide the core threads along the outline as you stitch them to the fabric. Keep the stitches close together to cover the core threads completely.

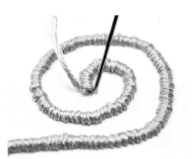

4 To finish, trim the core threads and work a couple more stitches to hide the ends. Pull the working thread to the back and secure it with a knot.

WHIPPED BACK STITCH

Whipped back stitch is often used for outlines and lettering, giving a subtle level of dimension. When using more than one colored thread, it provides a lovely striped and intertwined look.

1 First, stitch your outline using back stitch (see page 17).

2 Thread the second color (if using) and bring the needle up through the same hole as for the start of the first stitch, at A. Then, slide the needle under the first stitch, at B, entering from the top, and pull the thread through.

3 Continue sliding the needle under each subsequent stitch, always in the same direction.

4 After looping the thread through each back stitch, take the needle and thread to the back of the fabric and secure it with a knot.

RAISED LEAF STITCH

Raised leaf stitch is a simple stitch with a big impact. You will need a 1-inch- (2.5-cm-) wide piece of cardstock for this stitch.

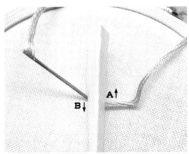

1 Fold the 1-inch- (2.5-cm-) wide cardstock in half so it creates a ½-inch (1.3-cm) tent shape. Place it, standing up, where the leaf will be.

2 Bring the needle up at A and down at B, creating a stitch around the cardstock. Repeat this with side-by-side stitches until you have six to eight loops around the card.

3 Slide the needle under the loops and pull through to the other side so the loops are around your working thread. Gently pull the cardstock away.

4 Guide the loops toward the direction of the stem. To form the leaf, take the needle and thread through the fabric at the point you want the stem to end. Secure the thread with a knot.

FRENCH KNOT

French knots can be used in isolation as decorative dots or grouped to fill in areas for textural impact. You can increase the size of the knot by wrapping the thread around the needle more times.

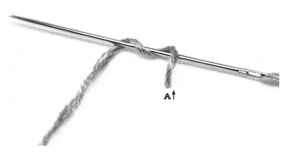

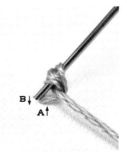

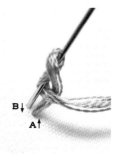

1 Bring the needle up at A. Wrap the thread around the needle twice and hold the working thread.

2 For a **tight** knot, hold the working thread taut and push the needle through the fabric at B, right next to A.

For a **loose** knot, hold the working thread loosely and push the needle through the fabric at B, right next to A.

3 Pull the needle all the way through and secure the thread on the back with a knot. A tight French knot (top) and a loose French knot (below) are shown.

DRIZZLE KNOT

A drizzle knot is a freestanding knot that provides dimension and texture. The technique is very similar to the casting-on technique used in knitting.

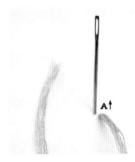

1 Bring the needle up through the fabric at A. Remove the thread from the needle. Place the point of the needle right next to the thread, pushing about a third of the way through the fabric.

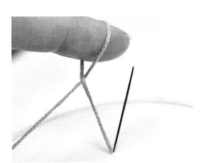

2 Place the working thread across your finger, nail side down. Then, twist your finger so your nail faces up, forming a loop. Slip the loop of thread from your finger onto the needle.

3 Slide the loop down to the base of the needle and pull the thread taut to tighten into a knot. Repeat steps 2 and 3 six to eight times.

4 Rethread the needle with the end of the working thread. Next, gently pull the needle through the knots to the back of the fabric, and secure the thread with a knot.

BULLION KNOT

A bullion knot is an incredibly versatile knot. It can be used as a single stitch for motifs such as petals or leaves, and multiple stitches can be layered to create highly textured flowers.

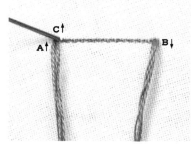

1 Bring the needle up at A and down at B. Bring the tip of the needle up at C, using the same hole as A. Do not pull the needle all the way through.

2 Gently wrap the thread around the needle. The number of wraps should cover the distance between A and B. For a curved bullion knot, the number of wraps should be greater than the distance between A and B.

3 Hold the wraps with your fingers and gently pull the needle and thread through, transferring from the needle to the working thread. Pull the working thread flush with the fabric as you slide the knot.

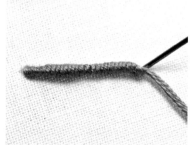

4 Take the needle down to the back of the fabric, using the same hole as B, and secure the thread with a knot.

RAISED CHAIN STITCH

Raised chain stitch is great to use for textured borders and wide curved lines. The look of the chain links can be varied by using fewer strands of thread or thicker yarns.

1 Using straight stitches (see page 16), create rows of evenly spaced horizontal stitches.

2 Bring the needle up through the fabric, above the middle of the top straight stitch. Slide the needle below the top stitch, from the bottom with the needle tip pointing up. Pull through.

3 Slide the needle under the same straight stitch, from the top with the needle tip pointing down. Tuck the free end of the thread under the needle, as shown. Pull through.

4 Repeat steps 2 and 3 for each subsequent straight stitch. After the last chain link, bring the needle to the back of the fabric and secure the thread with a knot.

LAZY DAISY STITCH

Lazy daisy stitch is stitched in a circle to create flowers and can be used singularly as leaves. You can vary the length of the loop and number of petals to make the daisies more versatile.

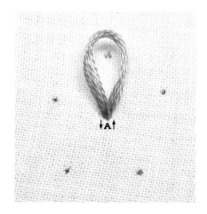

1 Bring the needle up at A. Then take the needle back down at A. Form a small loop, as shown.

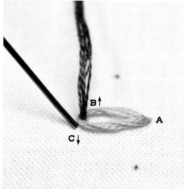

2 Bring the needle up at B. Shape the loop and secure the stitch by taking the needle down over the loop, at C.
*Two thread colors are used here to contrast each step, but the stitch can be completed with the same thread.

3 Repeat steps 1 and 2 until you have worked the desired number of petals.

TURKEY WORK

Turkey work is useful for adding velvety textures to embroidery. Often used to simulate hair or rugs when the loops are cut, the loops can also be left uncut for a woven look.

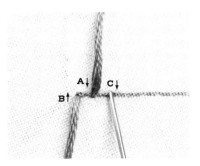

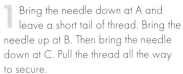

1 Bring the needle down at A and leave a short tail of thread. Bring the needle up at B. Then bring the needle down at C. Pull the thread all the way to secure.

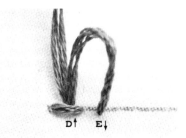

2 Bring the needle up at D, using the same hole as A. To create a short loop, bring the needle down at E.

3 Create a locking stitch to hold the loop securely in place by bringing the needle up at F, using the same hole as C. Then bring the needle down at G. Pull the thread all the way to secure.

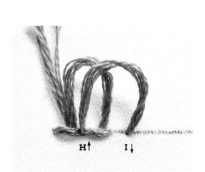

4 Bring the needle up at H and down at I. Continue this series of loops and locking stitches until the row is complete. Use scissors to cut each loop and trim the ends.

TASSEL STITCH

Tassel stitch gets its name because it resembles a tassel. It is often used to create fluffy three-dimensional flowers or to embellish the ends of stitched rugs.

1 Wrap a strand of thread around two fingers fifteen to twenty times. The more fingers used, the longer the final tassel. The more wraps, the fluffier the tassel will be.

2 Use a straight stitch (see page 14) to secure the wrapped thread to the fabric. The location of the straight stitch will be the base of the tassel.

3 Fold the loops over the straight stitch. Secure the base of the loops with a horizontal satin stitch (see page 20). Cover the base completely.

4 Use scissors to cut the exposed loops. Trim as needed.

BUTTONHOLE BAR

Buttonhole bar is a stitch that sits above the fabric. It can be used decoratively or as a way to connect two separate components.

1 Make two horizontal straight stitches (see page 16), one on top of the other. This will be the length of the finished buttonhole bar.

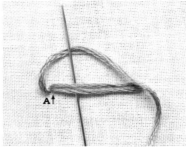

2 Bring the needle up through A. Then slide the needle under the two straight stitches. Tuck the working thread under the needle and pull through.

3 Repeat step 2 until the length of the straight stitches is covered.

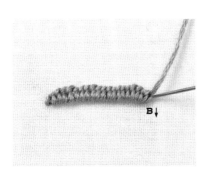

4 After reaching the end of the bar, bring the needle down at B and secure the thread on the back with a knot.

RAISED STEM BAND

Raised stem band uses a series of simple loops to give a highly textured look. It is used to fill in large areas, such as decorative borders, or to create stems and trunks.

1 Using straight stitch (see page 16), create a ladder of evenly spaced horizontal stitches. After the last straight stitch, bring the needle to the back of the fabric and secure the thread with a knot.

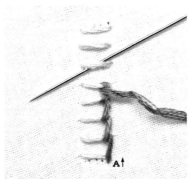

2 Thread the second color and bring the needle up at A. Entering from the top, slide the needle beneath the stitch above and pull through. Repeat until you reach the top straight stitch.

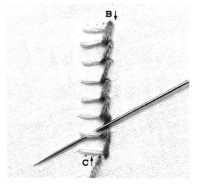

3 Bring the needle down to the back of the fabric at B, and bring the needle up next to the starting point, at C. Repeat steps 2 and 3 until the straight stitches are covered.

4 After covering all the straight stitches, bring the needle down at D and secure the thread on the back with a knot.

NEEDLE WEAVING

Needle weaving is weaving with needle and thread on the surface of the fabric. It is possible to create an even deeper dimension by using yarn in place of embroidery thread.

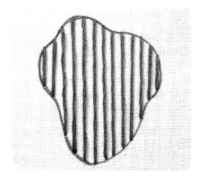

1 Using straight stitch (see page 16), create rows of evenly spaced vertical stitches that fill the entire shape. After the last straight stitch, bring the needle to the back of the fabric and secure the thread with a knot.

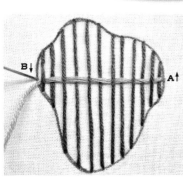

2 Thread the second color and bring the needle up at A. Without stitching into the fabric, use the needle to alternate an over-under weaving pattern through the vertical stitches. At the end of the line, bring the needle down to the back of the fabric at B.

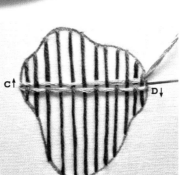

3 Bring the needle up at C to begin the next line. This time, alternate the over-under pattern with the previous line, as shown. At the end of the line, bring the needle down to the back of the fabric at D.

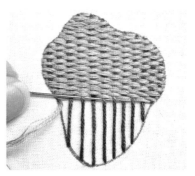

4 Continue weaving across the vertical stitches, using alternating over-under weaving until the area is covered. Use the needle to straighten each line as you go. To finish, secure the thread on the back with a knot.

NEEDLE WEAVING BAR

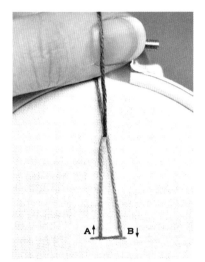

Needle weaving bar is a raised stitch that sits above the fabric. Vary the length and width of the stitch to create a variety of leaves, petals, tentacles, and tendrils.

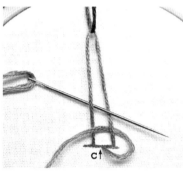

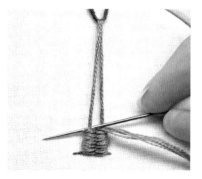

1 Bring the needle and working thread (pink) up at A and down at B. Do not pull all the way through. Use a scrap thread (green) to create a loop through the working thread and hold it with your thumb. Pull the working thread to the desired finished length of the bar.

2 Bring the needle up at C, still holding the scrap thread loop. Take the needle under the right side, over and under the left side, and back over the right side, as shown. Continue this figure-eight pattern all the way to the top of the bar.

3 Gently push the weaving down with the needle as you go along. Pull the thread firmly enough after each figure-eight to keep the weaving even.

4 After reaching the top of the loop, cut and remove the scrap thread. Bring your needle down to the back of the fabric and secure the thread with a knot. You can lay the bar flat or twist it for a raised effect.

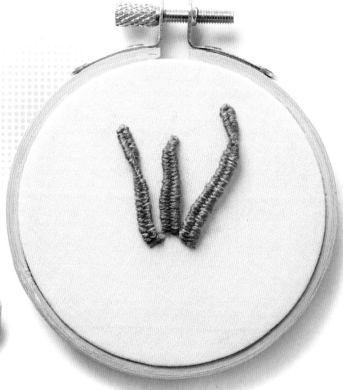

WOVEN PICOT

Woven picot is a freestanding stitch,
attached only at the base. Commonly
used for petals and leaves, it can be
layered to create three dimensional
flowers, succulents, or scales.

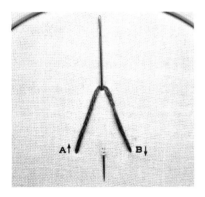

1 Place an anchor needle into the
fabric vertically, as shown. With a
second needle, bring the thread up at
A and down at B, wrapping the thread
around the top of the anchor needle.

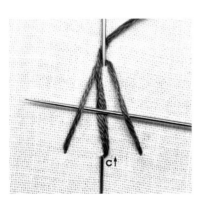

2 Bring the needle up at C and wrap
the working thread around the top
of the anchor needle. Without piercing
the fabric, weave across the three
vertical threads: under the first, over the
second, and under the third. Push the
weaving up to the top of the shape.

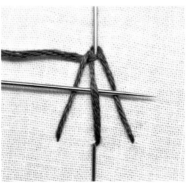

3 Next, weave in the opposite
direction: this time the needle goes
over-under-over. Continue weaving
across the vertical stitches in this way,
using alternating weaving patterns for
each row.

4 Use the needle to push each line
of thread upward as you weave.
After reaching the base, finish the stitch
by bringing the needle down to the
back of the fabric, at D, and secure
the thread with a knot. Gently slide the
anchor needle out of the fabric.

RAISED FISHBONE STITCH

Raised fishbone stitch uses overlapping stitches to create its raised look. It is most commonly used to create textured leaves of many shapes and sizes.

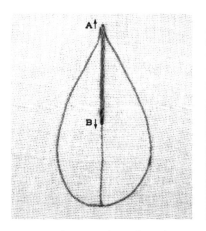

1 Start with a vertical straight stitch (see page 16) about half the length of the shape. Bring the needle up at A and down at B.

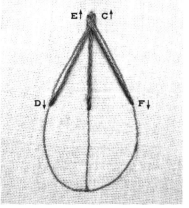

2 Next, bring the needle up at C and down at D, diagonally across the first stitch. Then, bring the needle up at E and down at F, creating another diagonal stitch in the opposite direction.

3 Continue the pattern of overlapping diagonal stitches as you work your way down the shape. After filling in the shape completely, bring the needle to the back of the fabric and secure the thread with a knot.

WOVEN WHEEL STITCH

Woven wheel stitch, also known as wagon wheel or rose wheel, is a popular raised stitch. It is most often used to create circular flowers, and the center can be filled in with decorative French knots.

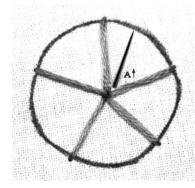

1 Work five evenly spaced straight stitches (see page 16), all meeting in the center of the circle. Then, bring the needle and thread up through the fabric at A, next to where the stitches meet.

2 Slide the needle through the straight stitches in an over-under weaving pattern. Continue until the straight stitches are completely covered.

3 To end the stitch, bring the needle to the back of the fabric and secure the thread with a knot. Use the eye of the needle to straighten or fluff the woven threads as needed.

RAISED CUP STITCH

Raised cup stitch uses a type of chain stitch that builds on top of itself. When worked with a smaller diameter, the finished stitch creates a berry-like dome. When made with a larger diameter, it creates a cup-like shape.

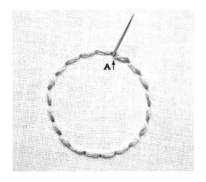

1 Use back stitch (see page 17) to stitch the outline of the base. Then, bring the needle up through the fabric at A, between two of the back stitches, and pull the thread through.

2 Slide the needle under the stitch to the right. Tuck the working thread under the tip of the needle and pull through. Repeat for each back stitch, creating a new layer of stitches.

3 Slide the needle under the first stitch of the new layer. Tuck the working thread under the tip of the needle and pull through. Repeat this step to continue building up layers to the desired number.

4 Weave the needle down the side of the cup, to the back of the fabric. Pull the thread through, being careful not to pinch the side, and secure the thread on the back with a knot.

PADDED SATIN STITCH

Padded satin stitch, like the flat satin stitch (see page 20), is used to fill in small to medium areas. It provides a smooth, slightly curved surface for a subtle dimension.

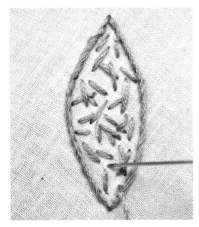  

1 Stitch the outline of your shape using stem stitch (see page 19). Next, begin to fill the inside of the shape using straight stitches (see page 16) in no particular pattern.

2 Add layers of straight stitches until you reach the desired height. Use up scrap threads for this since this layer will be covered over.

3 Using two strands of thread, use satin stitch (see page 20) to cover the base layer, making sure to stitch along the outside of the outline and cover the padding completely. To finish, secure the thread on the back with a knot.

FELT PADDED SATIN STITCH

Felt padded satin stitch provides a smooth, curved surface with a more pronounced dimension than padded satin stitch (see page 39). Use multiple layers of felt if you need to add more depth.

1 First, outline the shape with back stitch (see page 17) or stem stitch (pictured, see page 19).

2 Cut out a piece of felt to fit inside the shape of your outline. Secure the felt to the fabric with a straight stitch.

3 Take two strands of thread and use satin stitch (see page 20) to cover the felt padding completely, carefully following the outside of the outline. To finish, secure the thread on the back with a knot.

FELT PADDING

Felt padding is useful when creating a variety of levels within one shape. It uses layers of felt and can be covered with many different flat or raised stitches.

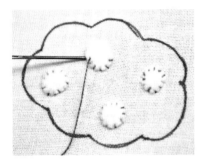

1 Cut the felt into very small versions of the shape needed. Attach them to the fabric by stitching along the edges, as shown.

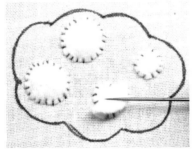

2 Cut more felt into slightly larger versions of the shape. Place them over the smaller pieces of felt. Attach them to the fabric by stitching along the edges. Continue adding layers of felt to increase the depth as required.

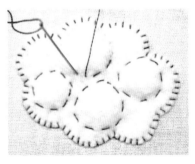

3 Cut out a final felt piece of the shape and size of the whole area. Attach the piece by stitching along the outside edges. Then, stitch around the humps created by the smaller felt layers.

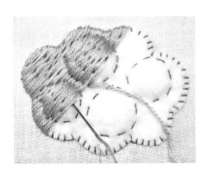

4 Use a full coverage stitch, such as satin stitch (see page 20), needle weaving (see page 33), needlelace (see page 45), or long and short stitch (pictured, see page 18) to cover the felt padding completely. To finish, secure the thread on the back with a knot.

TURNED EDGE SLIP

Turned edge slips require a separate piece of sturdy fabric to stitch the design on, like Aida cloth or canvas. Attaching the slip to the separate embroidery fabric is what gives it its raised look.

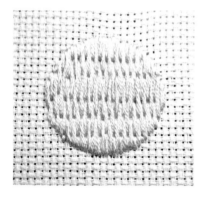

1 Stitch the design onto a thick, sturdy fabric (14-count Aida cloth is pictured here).

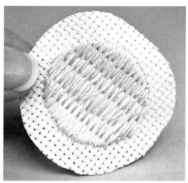

2 Cut out the shape, leaving about ¼ inch (6 mm) of fabric between the edge of the stitches and the edge of the fabric.

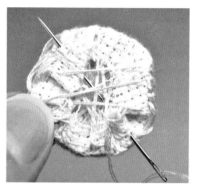

3 Turn the edges of the fabric slip inward, underneath the design. Stitch the turned edges closed at the back to hide and secure them, crossing from one side to the other.

4 Using one strand of thread, attach the slip to the embroidery fabric, stitching all the way around. If the slip indents or caves in when pushed, you can insert scrap threads or fabric under the slip before you finish attaching. To finish, secure the thread on the back with a knot.

WIRED SLIP

Wired slips require a separate piece of sturdy fabric, like Aida cloth or canvas, and thin flexible wire. Wired slips create a playful detached look and are often used for petals or wings.

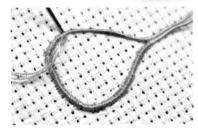

1 Bend the wire along the outline of your shape. Then, using two strands of thread, cover the wire completely with small stitches placed directly next to each other, like the ones used in overcast stitch (see page 21).

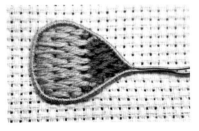

2 Fill the inside of the wired shape with your stitched design. Long and short stitch (see page 18) is pictured here.

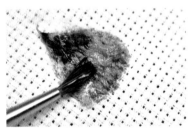

3 Apply a clear-drying glue to the stitches on the back of the fabric. Allow to dry.

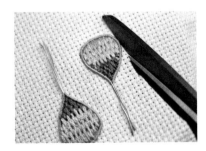

4 Using a sharp pair of scissors, cut the wired shape out. Hold the scissors at an angle so that you can position the blades as close to the wire as possible. Be careful not to cut the stitches.

5 Use the embroidery needle to poke a hole in the embroidery fabric where you would like the slip to sit. Then, push the uncut wires all the way through the fabric. Position the slip so that it sits in the direction you want it.

6 On the back side of the fabric, bend the wires to be parallel to the fabric. Stitch the wires to the fabric using one strand of thread that is the same color as the fabric. To finish, secure the thread on the back with a knot.

WRAPPED BEADS

Wrapping beads is a raised technique that provides strong pops of color and decoration to a design. You can use plastic beads, wooden beads, or even pearls and stones for this technique.

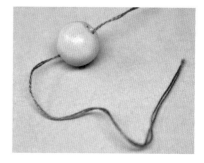

1 Thread the bead using two strands of thread. Cut the thread long enough to wrap the bead completely. Leave a 4–5-inch (10–13-cm) tail at the end.

2 Use the embroidery needle to neatly wrap the bead all the way around. If you run out of thread, tie another length of thread to the end close to the hole of the bead and trim.

3 After wrapping, leave a length of thread hanging from the other side of the bead. Thread the needle with both ends of the thread and bring the needle to the back of the fabric.

4 Position your bead and tie the two lengths of thread together on the back of the fabric.

NEEDLELACE

Needlelace provides a delicate lace effect to fill an area and lies above the fabric. While there are many different needlelace stitches, this single Brussels stitch is the most simple.

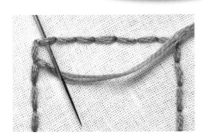

1 Outline the shape using back stitch (see page 17). Starting at the top left corner, without piercing the fabric, slide the needle under the top-left back stitch. Tuck the working thread under the tip of the needle and pull through.

2 Continue to slide the needle under each back stitch. Tuck the working thread under the needle tip each time to create loops. At the end of the row, bring the needle down to the back of the fabric at the top right corner, at A.

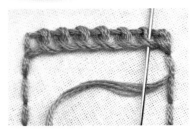

3 Bring the needle up where the next row will lie. Without piercing the fabric, slide the needle under the previous loops of the top row from the top. Tuck the thread under the needle tip and pull through each time.

4 At the end of the second row of loops, bring the needle down to the back of the fabric at B. Continue to work rows in this way until the shape is filled.

5 On the last row, slide the needle under each loop of the row above as well as the bottom outlined edge. Tuck the working thread under the needle tip each time and pull through.

6 After the final row is complete, bring the needle to the back of the fabric and secure the thread with a knot.

THE PROJECTS:
GETTING STARTED WITH RAISED STITCHES

CORD RAINBOW

Cord rainbows are a popular fiber arts project. This design uses a basic wrapping technique and one simple stitch to create a dramatic effect that gives a nod to the modern folk art aesthetic.

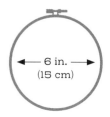

← 6 in. →
(15 cm)

Skill level

DMC colors

356
Medium terra cotta

758
Very light terra cotta

951
Light tawny

924
Very dark gray green

502
Blue green

Materials

- ○ Around 60 inches (1.5 m) of ⅛-inch (4-mm) macramé cord
- ○ 6-inch (15-cm) embroidery hoop
- ○ 8 x 8-inch (20 x 20-cm) piece of tan cotton fabric
- ○ Water-soluble or heat-sensitive marking pen
- ○ Embroidery needle
- ○ Scissors

Stitches used

- ○ Straight stitch (see page 16)

1 Cut the ⅛-inch (4-mm) macramé cord into five pieces, each measuring at least 12 inches (30 cm) in length.

2 Take one of the 12-inch (30-cm) cords and wrap it with your first thread color. Use the same method used for wrapping your hoop (see page 10). Measure 2 inches (5 cm) from the end of the cord and tie a knot with the end of the medium terra cotta thread. Wrap the thread for 8 inches (20 cm) and leave the last 2 inches (5 cm) unwrapped. Tie a knot and trim the ends.

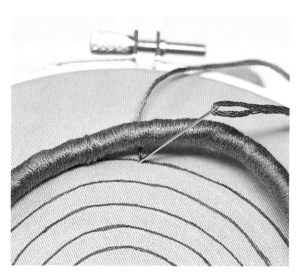

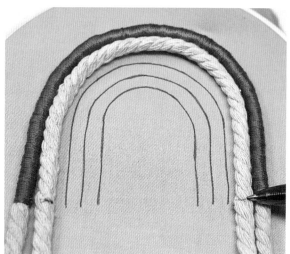

3 Lay the wrapped cord on the outer rainbow line with the knots facing the fabric. Thread the needle with medium terra cotta and bring the needle up to the front of the fabric at one end of the rainbow. Use straight stitches (see page 16) to stitch the cord onto the fabric.

4 Lay the next macramé cord on top of the fabric, beneath the first cord. Use a pen to mark where the thread wrapping should start and end. Wrap the cord with very light terra cotta thread.

5 Before tying the thread at the end of the cord, make sure the thread end is flush with the end of the pattern line. Then, use straight stitches to stitch it to the fabric. Repeat these steps for all remaining cords.

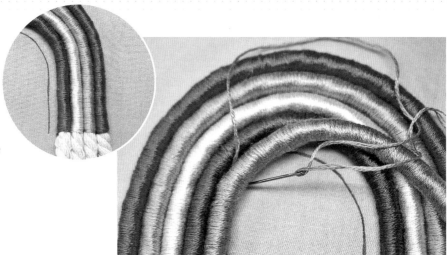

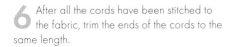

6 After all the cords have been stitched to the fabric, trim the ends of the cords to the same length.

7 Untwist the ends of each cord to turn it into a fringe. Use a needle to help brush out the strands.

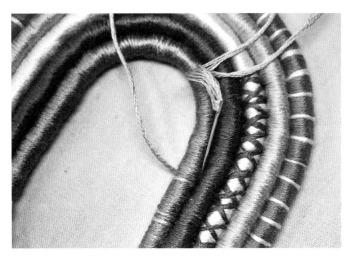

8 With the remaining thread, create patterns with straight stitches on the inner, middle, and outer cords. The outer cord shows evenly spaced straight stitches. The middle cord shows straight stitches crossed over each other to create a cross pattern. The inner cord shows two straight stitches close together, evenly spaced apart.

SUCCULENT IN A POT

This little succulent is created by adding layers of woven picot stitch. Wrapping the hoop provides a quaint potted look when the project is complete. Using different color palettes makes each succulent unique.

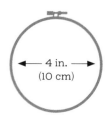

Skill level

DMC colors

772
Very light yellow green

524
Very light fern green

522
Fern green

780
Ultra very dark topaz

Materials

- ○ 4-inch (10-cm) embroidery hoop to stitch design
- ○ 3-inch (7.5-cm) embroidery hoop to frame design
- ○ 6 x 6-inch (15 x 15-cm) piece of tan cotton fabric
- ○ Water-soluble or heat-sensitive marking pen
- ○ Two embroidery needles
- ○ Scissors
- ○ Craft glue

Stitches used

- ○ Woven picot (see page 35)
- ○ Satin stitch (see page 20)

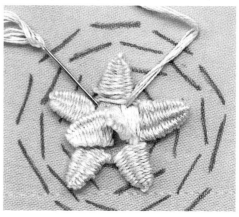

1 Stitch the design using a 4-inch (10-cm) hoop or larger. Begin the woven picot stitch (see page 35) on the two inner leaves with very light yellow green. Then stitch the five leaves around the inner two, in the same color thread. Place the anchor needle so each leaf measures around ½ inch (1.3 cm) long.

2 The fabric color may show between each leaf. Gently push the leaves to the side and use satin stitch (see page 20) to fill in the area using very light yellow green.

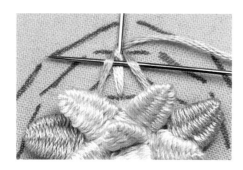

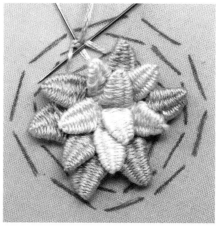

4 Use very light fern green to stitch the next layer of ½-inch (1.3-cm) leaves, which sit between the previous five leaves. Use satin stitch to fill in any gaps where the fabric shows through.

3 Using very light fern green, stitch the next five leaves in woven picot stitch. Place the anchor needle so each leaf again measures around ½ inch (1.3 cm) in length.

5 With fern green, stitch the next layer of nine leaves. Place the anchor needle so each leaf measures around ¾ inch (2 cm) long.

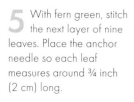

6 Use fern green to stitch the last layer of ¾-inch (2-cm) leaves, which sit between the nine leaves from the previous round. Use satin stitch in the same color thread to fill in any gaps where the fabric shows through.

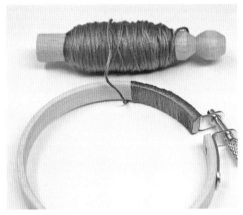

7 With ultra very dark topaz, wrap the outer part of the 3-inch (7.5-cm) hoop. Leave the thread on the bobbin and use craft glue to attach the end of the thread to one end of the hoop. Allow to dry. Tightly wrap the hoop, without gaps, and glue again when you've reached the other end. Allow to dry.

8 Remove the succulent from the 4-inch (10-cm) hoop and place it in the wrapped 3-inch (7.5-cm) hoop. Leave the outer hoop to sit slightly above the inner hoop to create the illusion of a flower pot.

DANDELION WISHES

The fuzzy texture in this design helps to create a scene reminiscent of warm summer evenings. It uses a combination of flat stitches and raised stitches to bring this dandelion to life.

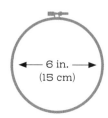

Skill level

DMC colors

 3031
Very dark mocha brown

 3013
Light khaki green

 ECRU
Off white

 420
Dark hazelnut brown

Materials

- ○ 6-inch (15-cm) embroidery hoop
- ○ 8 x 8-inch (20 x 20-cm) piece of peach cotton fabric
- ○ Water-soluble or heat-sensitive marking pen
- ○ Embroidery needle
- ○ Scissors

Stitches used

- ○ Stem stitch (see page 19)
- ○ Straight stitch (see page 16)
- ○ Overcast stitch (see page 21)
- ○ Turkey work (see page 29)

1 Use two strands of very dark mocha brown to stitch the outline of the face and hand with stem stitch (see page 19). Keep your stitches closer together on the more tightly curved lines. For the nails, use straight stitches (see page 16).

2 With light khaki green, use overcast stitch (see page 21) to complete all three sections of the stem on the dandelion. The interior threads can be any color.

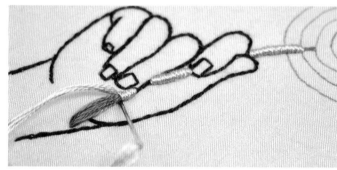

3 Stitch the rows on the flowered head of the dandelion with ecru off white, using turkey work (see page 29).

4 Again, use turkey work to create the floating seeds of the dandelion. Complete one turkey work loop for each line of the V at the top of each seed.

5 Cut the loops of each turkey work stitch on both the flowered head and the floating seeds. Then shape and trim the threads so they are even.

6 Finally, with two strands of dark hazelnut brown, stitch the stems of each floating seed with straight stitch (see page 16).

FLORAL MOTIF

The repeating pattern of these blooms is designed to encourage moments of mindfulness and a feeling of calm while stitching. These falling florals use all raised stitches and can be worked in several color palettes.

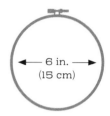

← 6 in. → (15 cm)

Skill level

DMC colors

 890
Ultra dark pistachio green

 35
Very dark fuchsia

 915
Dark plum

 550
Very dark violet

 561
Very dark jade green

Materials

- ○ 6-inch (15-cm) embroidery hoop
- ○ 8 x 8-inch (20 x 20-cm) piece of pale pink cotton fabric
- ○ Water-soluble or heat-sensitive marking pen
- ○ Embroidery needle
- ○ Scissors
- ○ Piece of card stock, measuring about ¼ inch (6 mm) tall when folded

Stitches used

- ○ Whipped back stitch (see page 22)
- ○ Lazy daisy stitch (see page 28)
- ○ Woven wheel stitch (see page 37)
- ○ Raised leaf stitch (see page 23)

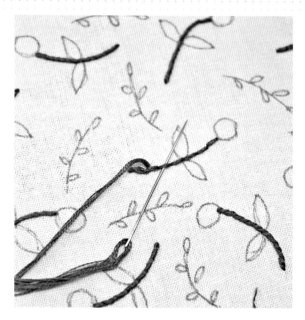

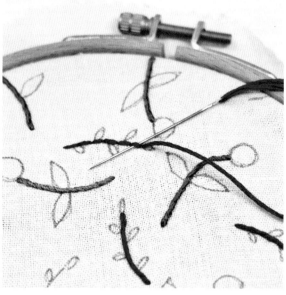

1 With ultra dark pistachio green, stitch the stems of each flower in whipped back stitch (see page 22).

2 With very dark fuchsia, stitch the stems of the leafy vines in whipped back stitch.

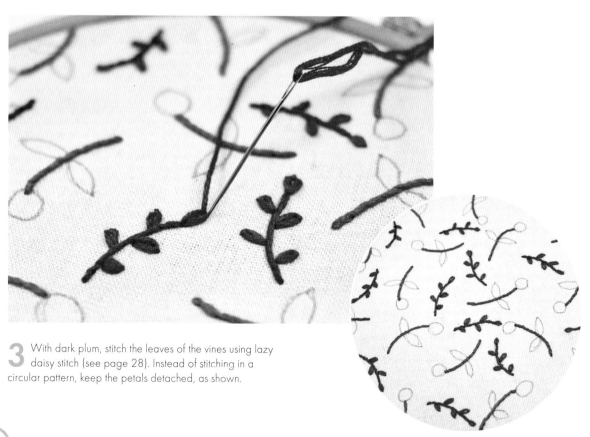

3 With dark plum, stitch the leaves of the vines using lazy daisy stitch (see page 28). Instead of stitching in a circular pattern, keep the petals detached, as shown.

4 On the circles for each of the flowers, work woven wheel stitch (see page 37) in very dark violet.

6 After pulling the needle through the loops, hold the working thread tight and bring the needle to the back of the thread right next to the stem. Vary the lengths of the stems to create a more organic look.

5 Stitch the leaves of the flowers in very dark jade green using raised leaf stitch (see page 23). Use a piece of card stock, measuring about ¼ inch (6 mm) tall when folded. Loop the thread around the cardstock four times. Push the needle through the loops facing away from the stem.

BUNCH OF BALLOONS

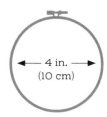

← 4 in. →
(10 cm)

Skill level

These pink and purple embroidered balloons add a touch of color and whimsy to any celebration. The raised balloons are given even more dimension with strings that hang straight off the hoop.

DMC colors

 433
Medium brown

 23
Apple blossom

 25
Ultra light lavender

 29
Eggplant

 32
Dark blueberry

 3064
Desert sand

 BLANC
White

Materials

- ❏ 4-inch (10-cm) embroidery hoop
- ❏ 6 x 6-inch (15 x 15-cm) piece of pale pink cotton fabric and fabric stabilizer
- ❏ Water-soluble or heat-sensitive marking pen
- ❏ Embroidery needle
- ❏ Scissors

Stitches used

- ❏ Back stitch (see page 17)
- ❏ Padded satin stitch (see page 39)
- ❏ Stem stitch (see page 19)
- ❏ Straight stitch (see page 16)

1 Stitch the outline of the arm with back stitch (see page 17). Use only one strand of medium brown thread. Make your stitches closer together on the curves of the fingers.

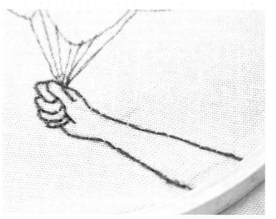

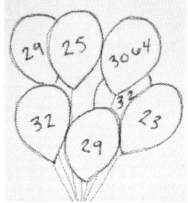

2 Plan out which thread colors you will use for each balloon. This image shows the DMC thread colors used in step 3.

3 Each balloon is worked in padded satin stitch (see page 39). First, stitch only the outline and inside padding for each balloon.

4 Then, complete the satin stitch covering using three strands of thread for each balloon. Stitching all the padding first will help to prevent any unwanted bunching or pulling on the surface of the balloons.

5 With one strand of thread, use stem stitch (see page 19) to outline each balloon. This helps to clean up the edges and defines each balloon. Start with the balloons in the back first, then stitch the balloons in the front.

6 Finally, use straight stitches (see page 16) with one strand of white to create the hanging strings. Start at the end of each balloon and bring each strand to the top of the hand, stitching through to the back side of the fabric. Then bring the thread to the front of the fabric at the bottom of the hand. Trim the ends of each thread to the desired length.

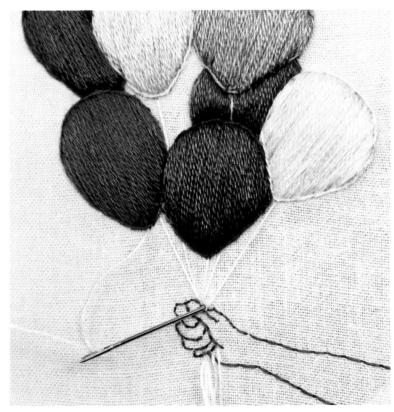

GLASS JAR BOUQUET

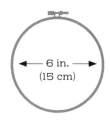

← 6 in. →
(15 cm)

Skill level

This minimal design sets a chic scene of freshly picked flowers. The flat stitches that imitate a vase create a perfect contrast with the raised stitches used for the flowers.

DMC colors

828
Ultra very light blue

830
Dark golden olive

371
Mustard

3045
Dark yellow beige

3022
Medium brown gray

3771
Ultra very light terra cotta

ECRU
Off white

Materials

- 6-inch (15-cm) embroidery hoop
- 8 x 8-inch (20 x 20-cm) square of 100% cotton fabric
- Medium-weight cut away fabric stabilizer
- Embroidery needle
- Scissors
- Water soluble or heat sensitive marking pen

Stitches used

- Back stitch (see page 17)
- Stem stitch (see page 19)
- Straight stitch (see page 16)
- Raised fishbone stitch (see page 36)
- Bullion knot (see page 26)
- Tassel stitch (see page 30)

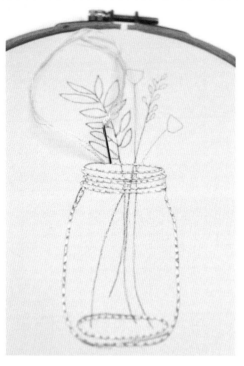

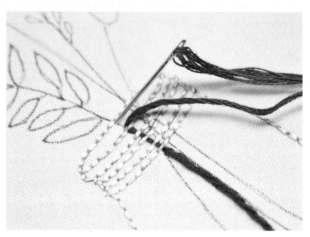

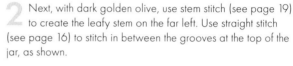

2 Next, with dark golden olive, use stem stitch (see page 19) to create the leafy stem on the far left. Use straight stitch (see page 16) to stitch in between the grooves at the top of the jar, as shown.

1 Using three strands of ultra very light blue, stitch the outline of the glass jar in back stitch (see page 17).

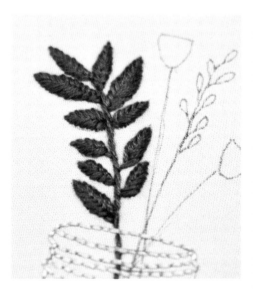

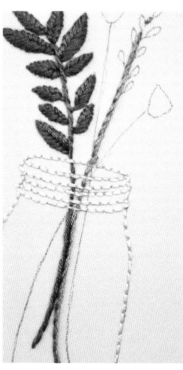

4 With mustard, use stem stitch to create the second to last stem of the bouquet. Again, use straight stitches to stitch between the grooves of the jar.

3 Then, use dark golden olive to stitch the leaves using raised fishbone stitch (see page 36).

5 Use dark yellow beige to create bullion knots (see page 26) to finish the leaves attached to the stem from step 4.

6 Work the remaining two stems in the jar with medium brown gray and stem stitch (see page 19). Remember to use straight stitch between the grooves of the jar.

7 Use tassel stitch (see page 30) to complete the flower on the far right. Combine all six strands of ultra very light terra cotta and all six strands of off white to make the tassel. Wrap the combined thread five times around two fingers. Then, secure the tassel with off white.

8 Create the final flower with tassel stitch. This time, use all six strands of off white and wrap the thread around two fingers ten times.

PUT YOUR HAIR UP

Grab a ponytail holder and get ready to create layers of dimension with incredibly fluffy textures. This design is great for showing off turkey work in three different ways.

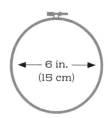

6 in. (15 cm)

Skill level

DMC colors

3371
Black brown

967
Very light apricot

524
Very light fern green

167
Very dark yellow beige

Materials

- 6-inch (15-cm) embroidery hoop
- 8 x 8-inch (20 x 20-cm) piece of light green cotton fabric
- Water-soluble or heat-sensitive marking pen
- Embroidery needle
- Scissors

Stitches used

- Stem stitch (see page 19)
- Turkey work (see page 29)
- Long and short stitch (see page 18)
- Satin stitch (see page 20)

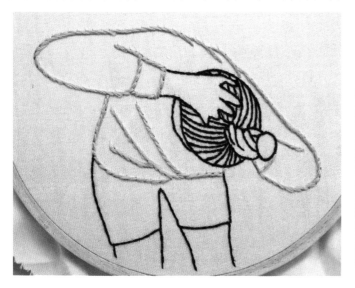

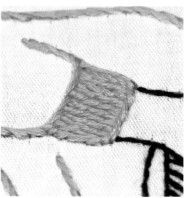

1 With two strands of black brown, use stem stitch (see page 19) to stitch the outline of everything except for the sweater. For the outline of the sweater, use stem stitch with six strands of very light apricot.

2 Next, fill in the cuffs of the sleeves. Use rows of stem stitch with six strands of very light apricot.

3 Fill the sweater in using rows of turkey work (see page 29) with six strands of very light apricot. The closer together you position your stitches, the more dense the fluff of the sweater will be once the threads are cut.

4 For the shorts, use long and short stitch (see page 18) with six strands of very light fern green. Start at the bottom of the shorts and work your way up to the top.

5 Using two strands of very dark yellow beige, fill in the legs, hands, and face with satin stitch (see page 20). You will not need to stitch the outline of the satin stitch first.

6 For the hair on the head, use turkey work with four strands of black brown. Make the loops of your stitches wide and sitting closer to the fabric. Overlap and vary the length and height of each stitch as you fill in each section.

7 Use six strands of black brown and turkey work stitch (see page 29) to create the ponytail. This time, keep your stitches very close together and make the loops as long as you would like the length of the ponytail to be.

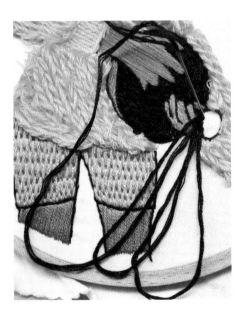

8 Use scissors to cut the loops of the sweater and the ponytail. Once the loops are cut, brush out the threads with the eye of your needle or a comb. Then, trim the threads of the sweater to an even length. For added dimension, leave the length on the arm slightly longer than the rest of the sweater.

POTTED PLANTS

This plant duo uses a mix of raised and flat stitches to help bring some lush plant-like foliage to the indoors. Enjoy creating those bold monstera leaves by using raised leaf stitch on a much larger scale.

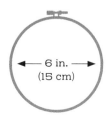

6 in.
(15 cm)

Skill level

DMC colors

 400
Dark mahogany

 167
Very dark yellow beige

 935
Dark avocado green

 367
Dark pistachio green

 3371
Black brown

 371
Mustard

Materials

- ○ 6-inch (15-cm) embroidery hoop
- ○ 8 x 8-inch (20 x 20-cm) piece of olive green cotton fabric
- ○ Water-soluble or heat-sensitive marking pen
- ○ Embroidery needle
- ○ Scissors
- ○ 5-inch- (13-cm-) wide piece of cardstock

Stitches used

- ○ Long and short stitch (see page 18)
- ○ Needle weaving (see page 33)
- ○ Satin stitch (see page 20)
- ○ Raised stem band (see page 32)
- ○ Needle weaving bar (see page 34)
- ○ French knot (see page 24)
- ○ Raised leaf stitch (see page 23)

 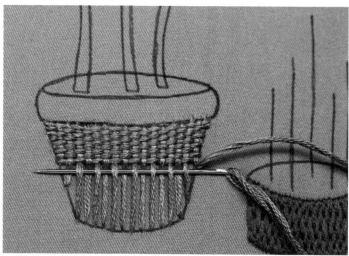

1 With six strands of dark mahogany, use long and short stitch (see page 18) to fill in the small pot on the right of the design.

2 Using six strands of very dark yellow beige, fill in the base of the pot on the left with needle weaving (see page 33). Then, use satin stitch (see page 20) to fill in the rim of the pot, also using six strands of very dark yellow beige.

3 Use raised stem band (see page 32) to stitch the stalks of the plant on the left of the design. Use six strands of dark avocado green.

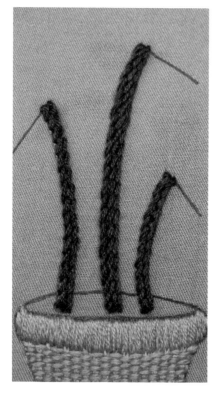

4 For the plant on the right of the design, use six strands of dark pistachio green and needle weaving bar (see page 34) to create the long leaves. Before stitching the top of the woven bar to the fabric, twist the bar slightly to give it a more organic look.

5 For both potted plants, use six strands of black brown to create the textured soil with French knots (see page 24).

6 For the leaves of the plant on the left of the design, you will use raised leaf stitch (see page 23). Fold the 5-inch (13-cm) piece of cardboard in half so it measures 2 ½ inches (6.5 cm) tall. Then, combine six strands of both dark avocado green and mustard and stitch around the cardstock about ten to twelve times, or the length of the detached line next to the stalk.

ABSTRACT DESERT

This embroidery design makes a great project to practice multiple raised stitches in a fun and easy sampler. The abstract elements include palm trees, cacti, water mirages, and drizzling rain drops.

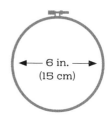

Skill level

DMC colors

926
Medium gray green

400
Dark mahogany

936
Very dark avocado green

436
Tan

433
Medium brown

3052
Medium green gray

3064
Desert sand

Materials

- ◯ 6-inch (15-cm) embroidery hoop
- ◯ 8 x 8-inch (20 x 20-cm) piece of lime green cotton fabric
- ◯ Water-soluble or heat-sensitive marking pen
- ◯ Embroidery needle
- ◯ Scissors

Stitches used

- ◯ Drizzle knot (see page 25)
- ◯ French knot (see page 24)
- ◯ Tassel stitch (see page 30)
- ◯ Bullion knot (see page 26)
- ◯ Raised chain stitch (see page 27)
- ◯ Buttonhole bar (see page 31)
- ◯ Back stitch (see page 17)

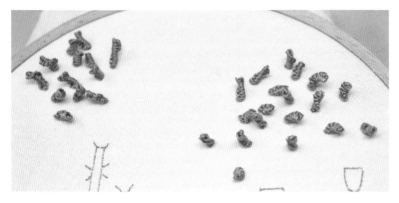

1 Using six strands of medium gray green, stitch a drizzle knot (see page 25) on each dot of the two patches at the top of the design.

2 Next, use six strands of dark mahogany to stitch a French knot (see page 24) on each circle of the two patches at the bottom of the design. Keep your thread loose as you pull the needle through to keep the knots loose.

3 With tassel stitch (see page 30), fill in the three cup shapes on the right side of the design. Use six strands of very dark avocado green and wrap the thread around two fingers, ten times. Then, use six strands of tan thread to secure them to the fabric.

4 Below the tassels, stitch long bullion knots (see page 26) with six strands of medium brown. As you wrap the thread around the needle, make sure the length of the bullion knot covers the length of the line.

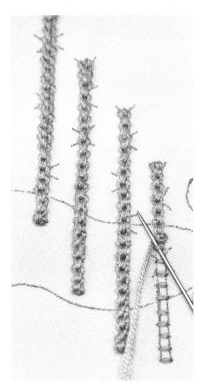

5 With six strands of medium green gray, cover each of the four rectangular trunks on the left of the design with raised chain stitch (see page 27).

6 Next, attach loops to the trunks using buttonhole bar (see page 31). For the side loops, use six strands of medium green gray. For the top loop of each trunk, use six strands of desert sand.

7 To complete the scene, use back stitch (see page 17) with six strands of medium gray green to outline the two organic shapes at the base of the design.

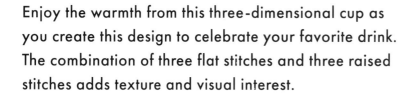
MORNING CUP OF COFFEE

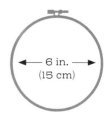
← 6 in. →
(15 cm)

Skill level

Enjoy the warmth from this three-dimensional cup as you create this design to celebrate your favorite drink. The combination of three flat stitches and three raised stitches adds texture and visual interest.

DMC colors

 310
Black

3778
Light terra cotta

 433
Medium brown

BLANC
White

 422
Light hazelnut brown

 167
Very dark yellow beige

 504
Very light blue green

 948
Very light peach

Materials

- 6-inch (15-cm) embroidery hoop
- 8 x 8-inch (20 x 20-cm) piece of aqua green cotton fabric
- Water-soluble or heat-sensitive marking pen
- Embroidery needle
- Scissors

Stitches used

- Stem stitch (see page 19)
- Satin stitch (see page 20)
- Back stitch (see page 17)
- Raised cup stitch (see page 38)
- Padded satin stitch (see page 39)
- Turkey work (see page 29)

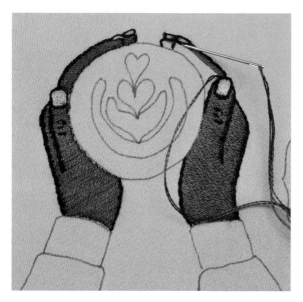

1 Outline the hands with stem stitch (see page 19) using two strands of black. Next, fill in the fingernails with satin stitch (see page 20) using two strands of light terra cotta. Then, fill in the hands using satin stitch and two strands of medium brown.

2 For the coffee cup, use six strands of white and stitch the outline with back stitch (see page 17). Then, use three strands of white and stitch the inner foam with satin stitch. With three strands of light hazelnut brown, stitch the rest of the coffee with satin stitch.

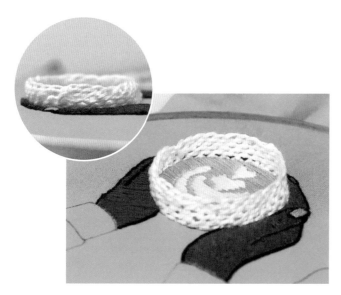

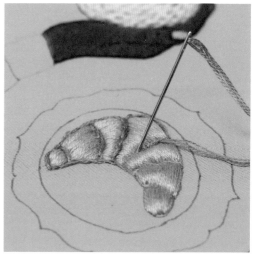

3 Add height to the coffee cup with raised cup stitch (see page 38). Using six strands of white, stitch at least five layers all the way around the cup. Keep the tension of the stitches as even as possible when working your way around.

4 To create the croissant, use padded satin stitch (see page 39) with six strands of light hazelnut brown. Stitch each triangular part separately, as shown. Then use three strands of very dark yellow beige to stitch the outline of the croissant with stem stitch.

5 Use six strands of very light blue green to stitch the outline of the sleeves with stem stitch. Then fill in the cuffs of the sleeves with rows of stem stitch.

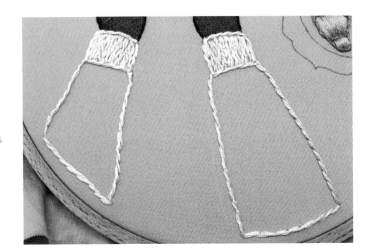

6 Use four strands of very light peach to stitch the outlines of the plate with stem stitch. Then fill in the plate with satin stitch using four strands of white.

7 To fill in the sleeves, use turkey work (see page 29) with six strands of very light blue green. Stitch rows from the bottom toward the cuffs, until the sleeves are filled. This time do not cut the loops of the turkey work stitches.

THE PROJECTS:

LEVEL UP WITH RAISED TECHNIQUES

I WANT CANDY

Let this gorgeous wildflowers coloris thread inspire you to create a tasty summer treat featuring a macramé cord lollipop. The macramé cord allows you to use the overcast stitch on a much larger scale.

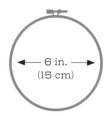

← 6 in. →
(15 cm)

Skill level

DMC colors

 4501
Wildflowers coloris

 3778
Light terra cotta

 758
Very light terra cotta

 948
Very light peach

BLANC
White

Materials

- 6-inch (15-cm) embroidery hoop
- 8 x 8-inch (20 x 20-cm) piece of light green cotton fabric
- Water-soluble or heat-sensitive marking pen
- 16 inches (40.5 cm) of ¼-inch- (6-mm-) wide macramé cord
- Embroidery needle
- Scissors

Stitches used

- Overcast stitch (see page 21)
- Back stitch (see page 17)
- Long and short stitch (see page 18)
- Raised stem band (see page 32)
- Straight stitch (see page 16)

2 Continuing with wildflowers coloris, begin working overcast stitch (see page 21) around the cord. Cover the ends of the cord completely and then continue stitching along the cord.

1 Using six strands of wildflowers coloris thread, stitch one end of the macramé cord to the middle of the lollipop swirl to secure it to the fabric.

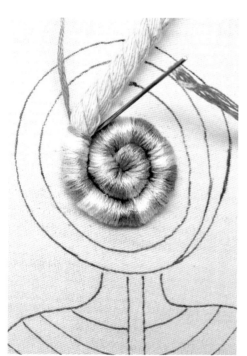

4 When you reach the end of the macramé cord, continue with overcast stitch until the end is completely covered.

3 Still working with wildflowers coloris, coil the macramé cord around itself using the swirl line as a guideline. Continue securing it to the fabric with overcast stitch.

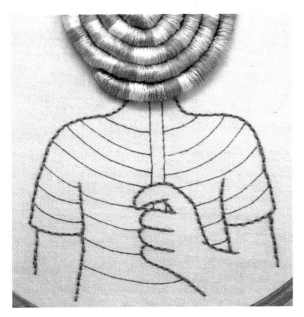

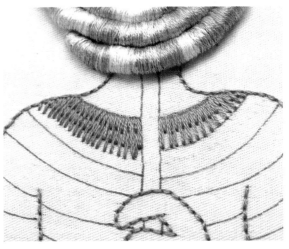

5 Next, use back stitch (see page 17) and three strands of light terra cotta to stitch the outline of the shirt, neck, and arms.

6 Using three strands of light terra cotta, use long and short stitch (see page 18) to begin filling in the top stripe of the shirt. The long stitch will be the width of the stripe, as shown on the right side of the shirt. Add a third row of long stitches, shown on the left side of the shirt, reaching halfway into the second stripe. Do this for both sides of the shirt.

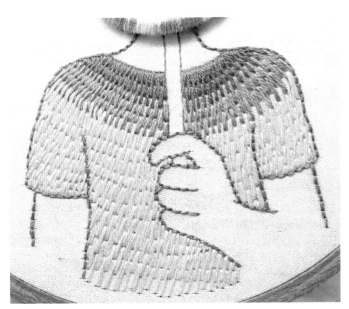

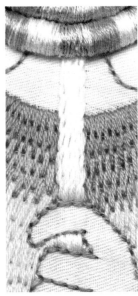

8 Finally, fill in the stick of the lollipop with raised stem band (see page 32) using white. For the small gap between the fingers, use straight stitches (see page 16).

7 Next, use three strands of very light terra cotta and stitch another three rows, continuing your long and short stitch work from step 6. After working those three rows, use very light peach to fill in the remainder of the shirt. Use the striped lines to help keep your stitches even.

BUNCH OF BLUEBERRIES

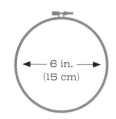

6 in.
(15 cm)

Create a sweet and tasty look with this branch that looks as though it was taken straight from a blueberry bush. After using the raised embroidery technique wrapped beads, you'll want to pluck one of these berries right off the hoop.

Skill level

DMC colors

938
Ultra dark coffee brown

890
Ultra dark pistachio green

823
Dark navy blue

Materials

- 6-inch (15-cm) embroidery hoop
- 8 x 8-inch (20 x 20-cm) piece of mint green cotton fabric
- Water-soluble or heat-sensitive marking pen
- Embroidery needle
- Scissors
- ¾-inch- (2-cm-) diameter wooden beads

Stitches used

- Overcast stitch (see page 21)
- Raised fishbone stitch (see page 36)
- Padded satin stitch (see page 39)
- Wrapped beads (see page 44)

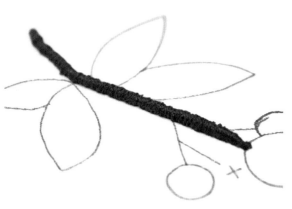

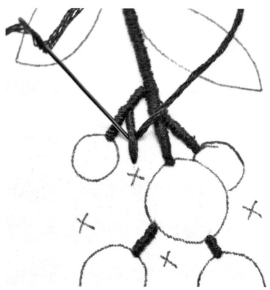

1 Use overcast stitch (see page 21) and stitch the main stem with six strands of ultra dark coffee brown. For the core threads, use four strands of any color thread.

2 Next, stitch the smaller stems attached to the main stem. Use overcast stitch with six strands of ultra dark coffee brown. For the core threads, use only two strands in any color thread.

3 On all four leaves, use raised fishbone stitch (see page 36) with six strands of ultra dark pistachio green thread. First stitch the two leaves layered behind, then stitch the two leaves in front.

4 For each of the blueberry circles, use padded satin stitch (see page 39) in dark navy blue thread. Use six strands for padding and two strands for the satin stitch.

5 Wrap the wooden beads using the wrapped beads technique (see page 44). Use two strands of dark navy blue for each bead.

6 Using the wrapped beads technique, attach the blueberries to the X marks on the design.

RECYCLED JELLYFISH

The relief in this jellyfish comes from layered felt padding and thread scraps. Made with recycled plastic bags, it gives a second life to what otherwise would be waste and reminds us to be mindful of our Earth and its resources.

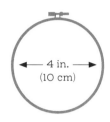

← 4 in. →
(10 cm)

Skill level

DMC colors

20
Shrimp

3778
Light terra cotta

543
Ultra very light beige

3810
Dark turquoise

3811
Very light turquoise

Materials

- ○ 4-inch (10-cm) embroidery hoop
- ○ 8 x 8-inch (20 x 20-cm) piece of green blue cotton fabric
- ○ Water-soluble or heat-sensitive marking pen
- ○ 8 x 8-inch (20 x 20-cm) piece of felt
- ○ Scissors
- ○ Thread scraps
- ○ Recycled plastic bag
- ○ Embroidery needle
- ○ Large-eye embroidery needle
- ○ PVA glue

Stitches used

- ○ Felt padding (see page 41)
- ○ Straight stitch (see page 16)
- ○ Stem stitch (see page 19)
- ○ Whipped back stitch (see page 22)
- ○ Needle weaving bar (see page 34)

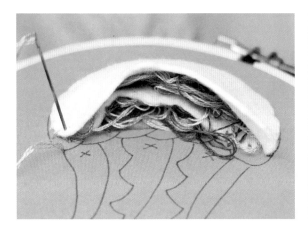

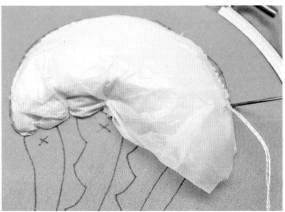

1 Use the felt padding technique (see page 41) for the body of the jellyfish. Cut out three pieces of felt in the shape of the jellyfish body, in decreasing sizes. For additional height, use thread scraps from your other embroidery projects and stuff them between each felt layer.

2 Cut a piece of your recycled bag in the general shape of the felt layers. Use straight stitch (see page 16) with two strands of any color thread to attach it. Fold and tuck the edges of the bag as you stitch to create a neat edge. The stitches along the top should be short and close together, creating a seam. Work only five to seven stitches along the bottom.

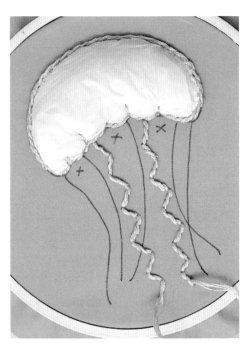

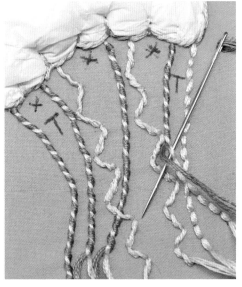

3 Use stem stitch (see page 19) with six strands of shrimp thread to outline the jellyfish body and the two zigzag tentacles. When you reach the end of the zigzag, bring the thread through the front of the fabric, cut, and let it hang freely.

4 Next, stitch the five remaining tentacles using whipped back stitch (see page 22) with six strands of both light terra cotta and ultra very light beige. Stitch the back stitch part with ultra very light beige. Stitch the whipped part with light terra cotta. At the end of each line, bring the thread through to the front of the fabric, cut, and let it hang freely.

5 Over the two Ts, create free-hanging tentacles with needle weaving bar (see page 34). Use six strands of both dark turquoise and very light turquoise. Thread the same needle with both colors of thread and weave as usual. At the end of the bar, cut and let the extra thread hang freely.

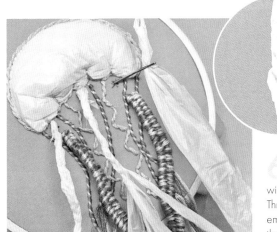

6 Over the three Xs, use 2-inch (5-cm) wide strips of plastic bag. Thread the large-eye embroidery needle with the tip of the bag and push the tip through the fabric. Then cut each strip into three strips and braid. Let the ends of each braid hang freely.

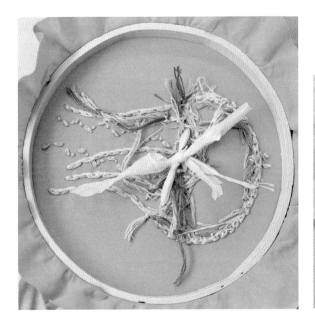

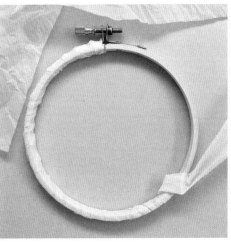

7 On the back of the hoop, secure the plastic bags by tying the ends of all three together.

8 Create a decorative frame using the same 4-inch hoop you used to stitch the design in. Cut the plastic bag into long strips, about 2-inch (5-cm) wide, and wrap the hoop, securing at intervals with craft glue. Use the same method as for thread wrapping (see page 10).

COZY IN BED

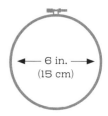

← 6 in. →
(15 cm)

Skill level

Create the perfect scene for a cozy night in bed. This design creates soft textures with needle weaving and flat stitches, and introduces the raised techniques of wired slips and felt padding.

DMC colors

371
Mustard

830
Dark golden olive

400
Dark mahogany

02
Tin oxide

924
Very dark gray green

168
Very light pewter

926
Medium gray green

Materials

- ○ 6-inch (15-cm) embroidery hoop
- ○ 8 x 8-inch (20 x 20-cm) piece of dark green cotton fabric
- ○ Water-soluble or heat-sensitive marking pen
- ○ Embroidery needle
- ○ Scissors
- ○ Felt
- ○ 24-inch (61-cm) length of 24-gauge (0.5 mm) wire

Stitches used

- ○ Stem stitch (see page 19)
- ○ Satin stitch (see page 20)
- ○ Back stitch (see page 17)
- ○ Long and short stitch (see page 18)
- ○ Felt padded satin stitch (see page 40)
- ○ Felt padding (see page 41)
- ○ Needle weaving (see page 33)
- ○ Wired slip (see page 43)

2 The table, teacup, and plant pot are all stitched with satin stitch and three strands of thread. The table is in dark golden olive. The plant pot is in dark mahogany. The tea cup is in tin oxide. The steam of the teacup is stitched with back stitch (see page 17) using three strands of tin oxide.

1 Use six strands of mustard to stitch the stem of the plant with stem stitch (see page 19). Then, use three strands of mustard to stitch the leaves of the plant with satin stitch (see page 20).

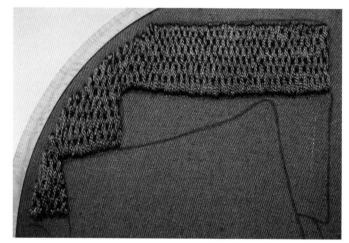

3 Stitch the headboard of the bed using six strands of very dark gray green. Complete the headboard using long and short stitch (see page 18).

4 The front pillow is stitched with felt padded satin stitch (see page 40). Begin by adding a layer of felt and securing it to the fabric. For added dimension, you can use the felt padding technique (see page 41).

5 Continue stitching both the front and the back pillows with satin stitch. Both pillows are worked in six strands of very light pewter.

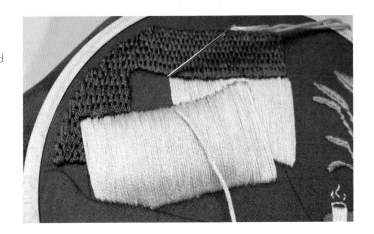

6 Stitch the outline of the blanket with six strands of tin oxide in back stitch. Use needle weaving (see page 33) to complete the blanket. Work the vertical stitches with six strands of medium gray green. Finish the needle weaving rows with six strands of tin oxide.

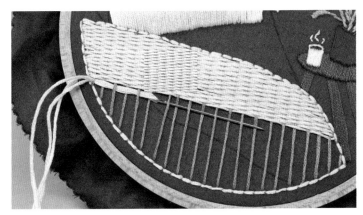

7 Fill in the bed sheets with satin stitch. Use three strands of medium gray green.

8 Finally, make the plant leaves pop up with the wired slip technique (see page 43). Choose three to four leaves to add the slips to. These wired slip leaves are worked in satin stitch, with three strands of mustard. When attaching the wire, use one strand of mustard thread and stitch around the stem of the plant to blend it in.

AT THE BEACH

This design is inspired by the joy of spending summer days at the beach. The raised stitches and turned edge slip used in this project create a straw hat and flip flops that look real enough to wear.

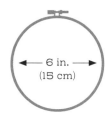

6 in. (15 cm)

Skill level

DMC colors

 437
Light tan

 310
Black

 17
Light yellow plum

BLANC
White

 351
Coral

Materials

- ○ 4-inch (10-cm) embroidery hoop
- ○ 6 x 6-inch (15 x 15-cm) piece of Aida cloth
- ○ Water-soluble or heat-sensitive marking pen
- ○ Embroidery needle
- ○ Scissors
- ○ 6-inch (15-cm) embroidery hoop
- ○ 8 x 8-inch (20 x 20-cm) piece of light blue cotton fabric

Stitches used

- ○ Turned edge slip (see page 42)
- ○ Back stitch (see page 17)
- ○ Satin stitch (see page 20)
- ○ Buttonhole bar (see page 31)
- ○ Straight stitch (see page 16)

1 Use the 4-inch hoop and Aida cloth to create a turned edge slip (see page 42). Transfer the circle labeled A from the pattern onto the Aida cloth. With six strands of light tan, work rings of back stitch (see page 17) to fill in the circle. Interlock the stitches with each new ring, to create a look similar to long and short stitch (see page 18).

2 Cut out the slip and attach it to the light blue fabric in the 6-inch (15-cm) hoop as for a turned edge slip. Use two strands of light tan and attach it to the inner circle of the hat on the pattern, also labeled A.

3 After attaching the slip, work rings of back stitch to create the brim of the hat. Use six strands of light tan and stitch the rings, starting at the edge of the slip and working outward. Again, create an interlocking pattern with the stitches of each new ring.

4 Next, stitch the small black sunglasses. Use satin stitch (page 20) with two strands of black.

5 Create the straps of the flip flops with buttonhole bar (see page 31). Use six strands of light yellow plum. The three dots of each flip flop on the pattern show where to place each of the straps.

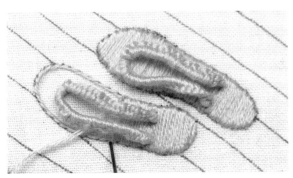

6 With two strands of light yellow plum, stitch the base of the flip flops in satin stitch. Carefully slide your needle under the buttonhole bar straps when stitching across the width of the shoes.

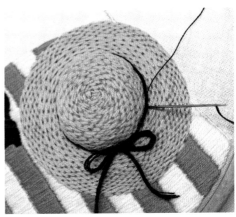

7 Stitch the stripes of the towel in satin stitch. Use two strands of white to stitch the outline. Then, create the red and white pattern with four strands of white and four strands of coral.

8 Finally, take six strands of black and tie a bow around the crown of the hat. Trim the tails of the bow to your desired length. To keep the bow in place, use one strand of black to place five evenly spaced straight stitches (see page 16) around the thread of the bow.

TOADSTOOL MUSHROOM

This toadstool design gets its charm from the felt padding and needlelace techniques. While it frames well in a hoop, it can also be the perfect embellishment to a canvas bag or throw pillow.

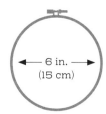

← 6 in. →
(15 cm)

Skill level

DMC colors

355
Dark terra cotta

3866
Ultra very light mocha brown

730
Very dark olive green

Materials

- ○ 6-inch (15-cm) embroidery hoop
- ○ 8 x 8-inch (20 x 20-cm) piece of felt
- ○ 8 x 8-inch (20 x 20-cm) piece of navy blue cotton fabric
- ○ Water-soluble or heat-sensitive marking pen
- ○ Embroidery needle
- ○ Scissors

Stitches used

- ○ Felt padding (see page 41)
- ○ Felt padded satin stitch (see page 40)
- ○ French knot (see page 24)
- ○ Needlelace (see page 45)
- ○ Needle weaving bar (see page 34)
- ○ Stem stitch (see page 19)

1. Trace and cut out the felt for both mushrooms using the felt padding technique (see page 41). Create layers for the mushroom caps and mushroom stalks separately. The larger mushroom is made with five layers for the cap and two layers for the stalk. The smaller mushroom is made with four layers for the cap and two layers for the stalk.

2. Using the felt padding technique (see page 41), attach each section of the felt layers to the fabric, starting with the smallest layers first and ending with the largest on top.

3. Next, cover the mushroom caps with felt padded satin stitch (see page 40). Use six strands of the dark terra cotta thread.

4. With six strands of ultra very light mocha brown, stitch about thirty tight French knots (see page 24) scattered around the large mushroom cap. Stitch about fifteen tight French knots scattered around the smaller mushroom cap.

5 Stitch the stalks of each mushroom with felt padded satin stitch. Use six strands of ultra very light mocha brown.

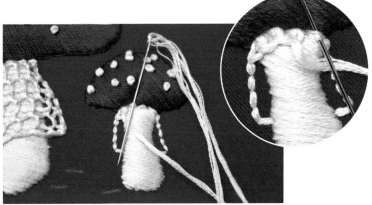

6 Stitch the two mushroom skirts with six strands of ultra very light mocha brown. Use the needlelace technique (see page 45) for both skirts. When stitching the back stitch outline, keep the top stitches relatively loose. Slowly work the needle through the back stitches to avoid snagging any threads.

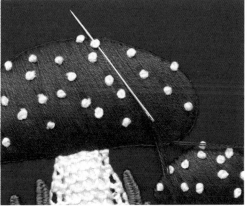

7 To create the grass, work needle weaving bars (see page 34) with six strands of very dark olive green. The five blades of grass around the large mushroom are about 1–1½ inches (2.5–4 cm) long. The three blades of grass around the small mushroom are about 1 inch (2.5 cm) long.

8 Finally, tidy up the mushroom caps. Use one to two strands of dark terra cotta to fill in any gaps in the satin stitch created by the French knots. Stitch through the French knot if needed. Then, use one strand of dark terra cotta and stem stitch (see page 19) to outline the mushroom caps.

FLORAL CROWN

Embroidered flowers are a classic motif in the world of embroidery and add sophistication to any project. With its delicate botanical flowers, this design is perfect for practice in combining multiple wire slips.

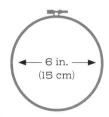

← 6 in. →
(15 cm)

Skill level

DMC colors

 433
Medium brown

 967
Very light apricot

 3773
Medium desert sand

 561
Very dark jade green

 368
Light pistachio green

 3820
Dark straw

 310
Black

Materials

- Two 6-inch (15-cm) embroidery hoops
- 8 x 8-inch (20 x 20-cm) piece of periwinkle blue cotton fabric
- Water-soluble or heat-sensitive marking pen
- Embroidery needle
- Scissors
- ½-inch- (1.3-cm-) wide piece of cardstock
- 8 x 8-inch (20 x 20-cm) piece of Aida cloth
- 30-inch (76-cm) length of 24-gauge (0.5-mm) wire

Stitches used

- Stem stitch (see page 19)
- Straight stitch (see page 16)
- Woven wheel stitch (see page 37)
- Whipped back stitch (see page 22)
- Raised leaf stitch (see page 23)
- Wired slip (see page 43)
- Satin stitch (see page 20)
- French knot (see page 24)

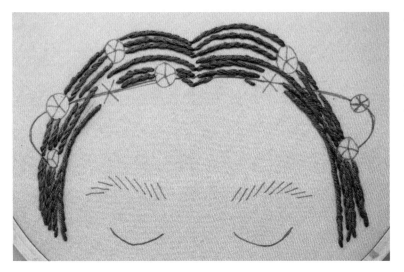

1 Stitch the hair using six strands of medium brown. Use stem stitch (see page 19) for each strand of hair, skipping over the symbols marked for the crown's flowers and leaves.

2 With six strands of medium brown, use straight stitch (see page 16) to stitch both of the eyebrows.

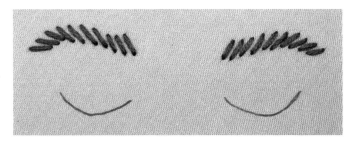

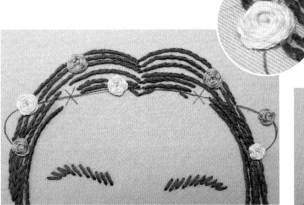

3 The seven circles along the crown are filled in with woven wheel stitch (see page 37). Use six strands of very light apricot to stitch three of the flowers. Use six strands of medium desert sand to stitch four of the flowers.

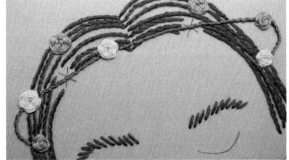

4 Create the crown stem with six strands of very dark jade. Complete the entire length of the stem with whipped back stitch (see page 22).

5 The leaves along the crown are marked with straight lines and are stitched with six strands of light pistachio green in raised leaf stitch (see page 23). Fold the cardstock in half so it is ¼ inch (6 mm) in height. Wrap the thread around the cardstock three to four times for each leaf.

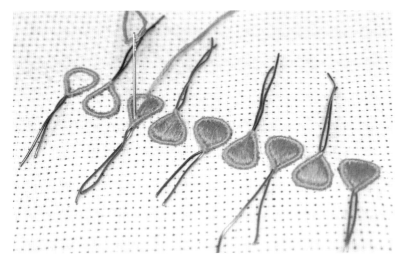

6 Transfer the flower petals from the pattern to the Aida cloth placed inside the second 6-inch (15-cm) hoop. Cut 3 inches (7.5 cm) of the wire for each petal and use the wired slip technique (see page 43). With three strands of the dark straw thread, fill in each petal with satin stitch (see page 20).

8 Finally, stitch both eyes with six strands of black, using whipped back stitch (page 22).

7 Using the wired slip technique, attach three of the petal slips to each X to form a flower. Use two strands of medium brown to attach the wires, stitching along the strands of hair to blend the threads in. Use six strands of dark straw and place a French knot (see page 24) in the middle of each flower.

THE PROJECTS:

BRINGING IT ALL TOGETHER

A DAY AT THE PARK

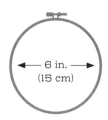

← 6 in. →
(15 cm)

A romantic scene that captures the essence of spring, this design features a beautiful landscape around a picnic basket. Use a combination of multiple raised and flat stitches to complete the scene.

Skill level

DMC colors

738
Very light tan

367
Dark pistachio green

819
Light baby pink

898
Very dark coffee brown

17
Light yellow plum

935
Dark avocado green

500
Very dark blue green

Materials

- 4-inch (10-cm) embroidery hoop
- 6 x 6-inch (15 x 15-cm) piece of Aida cloth
- Water-soluble or heat-sensitive marking pen
- Embroidery needle
- Scissors
- 6-inch (15-cm) embroidery hoop
- 8 x 8-inch (20 x 20-cm) piece of light blue cotton fabric

Stitches used

- Turned edge slip (see page 42)
- Needle weaving (see page 33)
- Long and short stitch (see page 18)
- Lazy daisy stitch (see page 28)
- Buttonhole bar (see page 31)
- Turkey work (see page 29)
- French knot (see page 24)
- Raised stem band (see page 32)
- Stem stitch (see page 19)
- Satin stitch (see page 20)

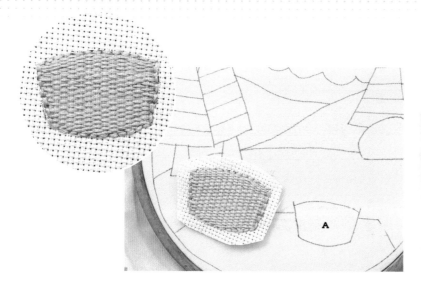

1 Use the 4-inch hoop and Aida cloth to create a turned edge slip (see page 42). Transfer the turned edge slip outline from the pattern, labeled A, onto the Aida cloth. Use needle weaving (see page 33) with six strands of very light tan to fill in the slip. Then cut out the slip.

2 Attach the slip to the picnic basket on the pattern, also labeled A. Use the turned edge slip technique with two strands of very light tan.

3 Long and short stitch (see page 18) is used for each of the following elements. The grass uses six strands of dark pistachio green with the stitches running horizontally. The blanket uses six strands of light baby pink with the stitches running vertically. The tree trunks use six strands of very dark coffee brown with the stitches running vertically.

4 On the pink blanket, create a floral design using lazy daisy stitch (see page 28). Stitch nine daisies scattered around the blanket with three strands of light yellow plum. Then, create the handle of the picnic basket with a buttonhole bar (see page 31). Use six strands of very light tan.

5 The three triangular trees use turkey work (see page 29). Use six strands of dark avocado green to complete each row. Keep the loops long enough to reach the row below. Trim the loops to an even length across each row.

6 Create both the bush at the right and the top of the floral tree in the middle of the pattern with French knots (see page 24). Stitch the treetop with six strands of light baby pink. Stitch the bush with six strands of very dark blue green, adding ten scattered French knots in light baby pink afterward.

7 The trunk and branches of the floral tree are worked in six strands of very dark coffee brown. Stitch the trunk in raised stem band (see page 32) and the branches in stem stitch (see page 19).

8 Stitch the hill in the background in satin stitch (see page 20). Use three strands of very dark blue green.

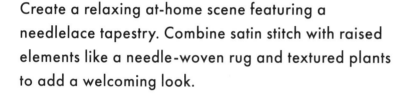

AN AFTERNOON AT HOME

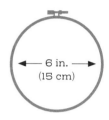

← 6 in. (15 cm) →

Skill level

Create a relaxing at-home scene featuring a needlelace tapestry. Combine satin stitch with raised elements like a needle-woven rug and textured plants to add a welcoming look.

DMC colors

310
Black

924
Very dark gray green

780
Ultra very dark topaz

BLANC
White

436
Tan

738
Very light tan

500
Very dark blue green

Materials

- 6-inch (15-cm) embroidery hoop
- 8 x 8-inch (20 x 20-cm) piece of pale blue cotton fabric
- Water-soluble or heat-sensitive marking pen
- Two embroidery needles
- Scissors
- 4 x 4-inch (10 x 10-cm) piece of felt

Stitches used

- Stem stitch (see page 19)
- Felt padded satin stitch (see page40)
- Overcast stitch (see page 21)
- Satin stitch (see page 20)
- Needle weaving (see page 33)
- Needlelace (see page 45)
- Turkey work (see page 29)
- Straight stitch (see page 16)
- Woven picot (see page 35)

1 Using two strands of black thread, stitch the outline of the pattern in stem stitch (see page 19). Do not stitch the legs of the chair or the rectangular tapestry.

2 Stitch the pillow on the chair with felt padded satin stitch (see page 40). Use three strands of very dark gray green and stitch diagonally across the pillow. Keep the stitches inside the black outline.

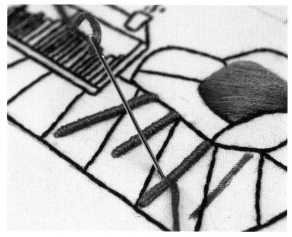

3 To stitch the legs of the chair, use overcast stitch (see page 21) with six strands of ultra very dark topaz. For the core threads, use three strands of any color thread.

4 Satin stitch (see page 20) is used for each of the following elements. The chair uses six strands of white. The floor uses six strands of tan. The bookshelf uses three strands of ultra very dark topaz. The tea cup and plant pot A use three strands of white. The books on the shelf use three strands of the colors of your choice. Keep the satin stitches inside the black outlines.

5 Stitch the rug with six strands of very dark gray green. Stitch plant pot B with six strands of very light tan. Use needle weaving (see page 33) to complete both, keeping the woven stitches inside the black outlines.

6 The woven tapestry on the wall is completed with the needlelace technique (see page 45). Use six strands of white. Place twelve back stitches along the top and bottom lines and six back stitches along the sides. For a tighter weave, increase the number of back stitches.

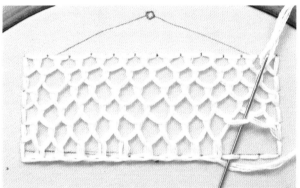

8 In plant pot A, create the three leaves of the plant with woven picot (see page 35). In plant pot B, create the grassy leaves with a row of turkey work and trim the loops. Use six strands of very dark blue green for both plants.

7 To complete the woven tapestry, use six strands of white to stitch one row of turkey work (see page 29) along the bottom edge. Trim the loops to create the fringe. Then, use two straight stitches (see page 16) to create the string the tapestry is hung by.

DINING OUT

This embroidered ramen noodle bowl features wired slip chopsticks in combination with a variety of raised and flat stitches. The result is a delightful dinner-themed piece to add to your hand-crafted collection.

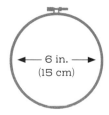

6 in.
(15 cm)

Skill level

DMC colors

 310
Black

 938
Ultra dark coffee brown

 976
Medium golden brown

BLANC
White

 3046
Medium yellow beige

 894
Very light carnation

 433
Medium brown

 436
Tan

 422
Light hazelnut brown

 3348
Light yellow green

 3777
Very dark terra cotta

Materials

- 6-inch (15-cm) embroidery hoop
- 8 x 8-inch (20 x 20-cm) piece of royal blue cotton fabric
- Water-soluble or heat-sensitive marking pen
- Embroidery needle
- Scissors
- 6 x 6-inch (15 x 15-cm) piece of felt
- 4-inch (10-cm) embroidery hoop
- 6 x 6-inch (15 x 15-cm) piece of Aida cloth
- 12-inch (30-cm) length of 24-gauge (0.5-mm) wire

Stitches used

- Stem stitch (see page 19)
- Back stitch (see page 17)
- Raised stem band (see page 32)
- Padded satin stitch (see page 39)
- Satin stitch (see page 20)
- Overcast stitch (see page 21)
- Felt padded satin stitch (see page 40)
- French knot (see page 24)
- Wired slip (see page 43)

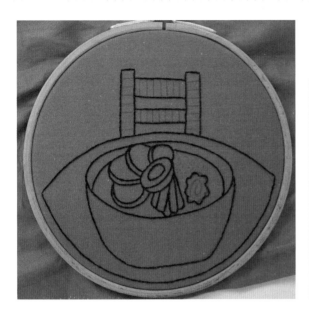

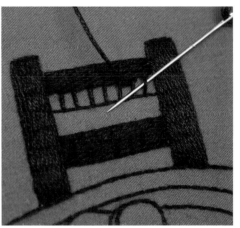

1 Use stem stitch (see page 19) or back stitch (see page 17) to stitch the outline of the chair, bowl, table, and ingredients. Use two strands of black. Do not stitch the swirled line inside the narutomaki fish cake.

2 With six strands of ultra dark coffee brown, use raised stem band (see page 32) to stitch each section of the chair. Keep the stitches inside the black outline.

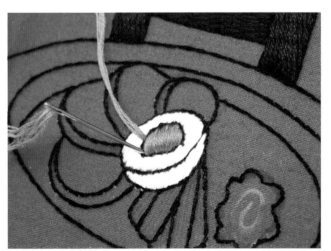

3 Stitch the hard-boiled egg next. For the egg yolk, use padded satin stitch (see page 39) with six strands of medium golden brown. For the egg whites, use satin stitch (see page 20) with four strands of white. Keep the stitches inside the black outlines.

4 Next, stitch the bamboo shoots and the narutomaki fish cake. Fill in the bamboo using rows of stem stitch with six strands of medium yellow beige. For the fish cake, stitch the swirl with six strands of very light carnation in stem stitch. Then, fill in the rest of the fish cake with six strands of white in satin stitch.

5 Stitch the six exposed noodles with overcast stitch (see page 21) using six strands of white. Then stitch the four pieces of pork. Stitch the seared edge with three strands of medium brown in satin stitch. Then fill in each slice of pork with three strands of tan and felt padded satin stitch (see page 40).

6 Fill the inside of the bowl with broth using four strands of light hazelnut brown and satin stitch. Then, with six strands of light yellow green, stitch the scallions. Place twenty loose French knots (see page 24) roughly where the black dots are shown on the pattern.

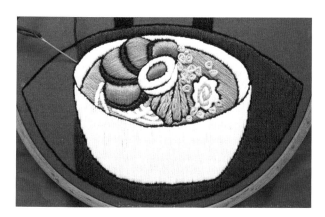

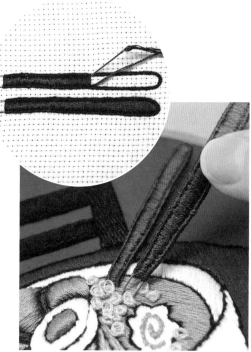

7 Fill in the bowl and the tablecloth with satin stitch. For the bowl, use six strands of white. For the tablecloth, use six strands of very dark terra cotta.

8 Transfer the chopsticks from the pattern onto the Aida cloth placed inside the 4-inch (10-cm) hoop. Use the wired slip technique (see page 43) with two strands of medium brown. Fill in the chopsticks with satin stitch, using three strands of medium brown. Each chopstick uses 6 inches (15 cm) of wire. Place the chopsticks on the points labeled T on the transfer pattern.

TEMPLATES

On these pages you will find templates for all the designs in the book. Start by enlarging the required template by 150 percent on a photocopier and then follow the instructions on page 13 to transfer the design to the fabric. The templates can also be found at full size on the iron-on transfer sheets in the envelope at the back of the book (see page 13 for instructions).

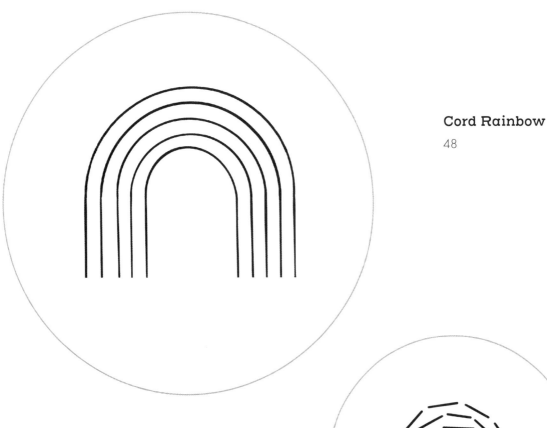

Cord Rainbow

48

Succulent in a Pot

52

Dandelion Wishes

56

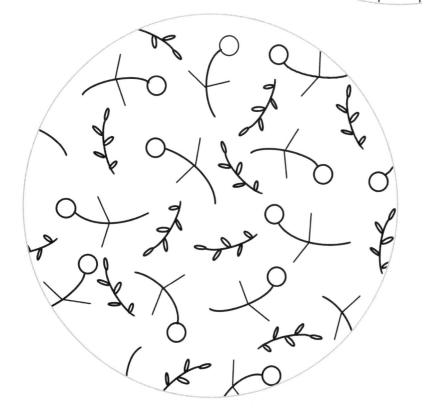

Floral Motif

60

Bunch of Balloons

64

**Glass Jar
Bouquet**

68

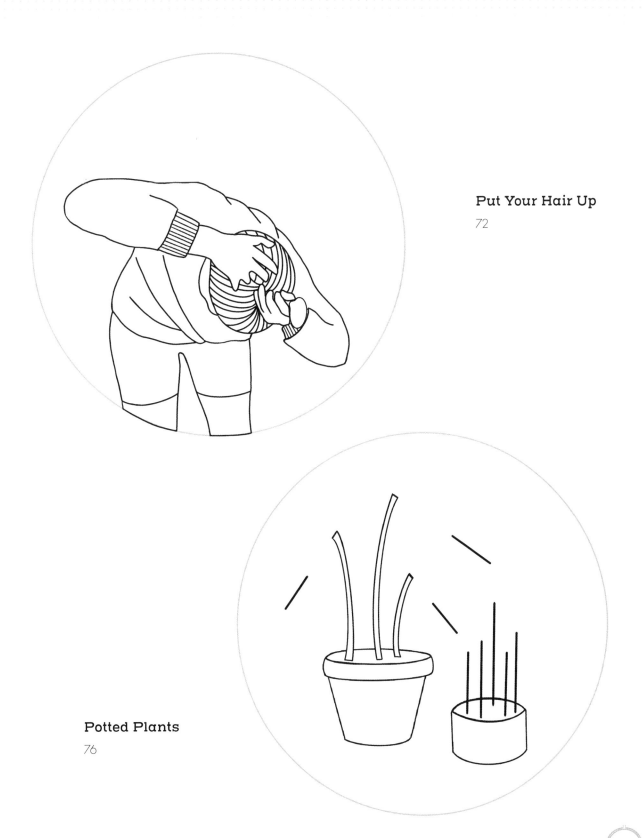

Put Your Hair Up

72

Potted Plants

76

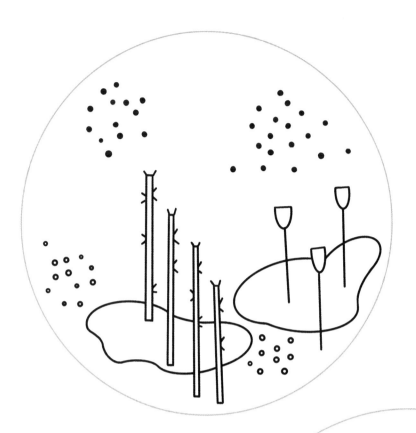

Abstract Desert
80

**Morning Cup
of Coffee**
84

I Want Candy

90

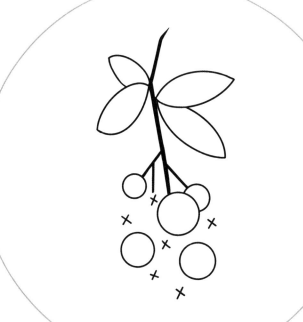

**Bunch of
Blueberries**

94

Recycled Jellyfish

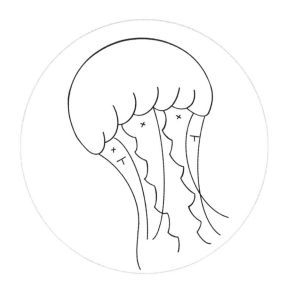

Cozy in Bed

At the Beach
106

A

Turned
edge slip

**Toadstool
Mushroom**
110

Floral Crown
114

Wired slips

A Day at the Park
120

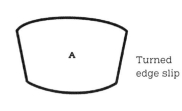

Turned
edge slip

A

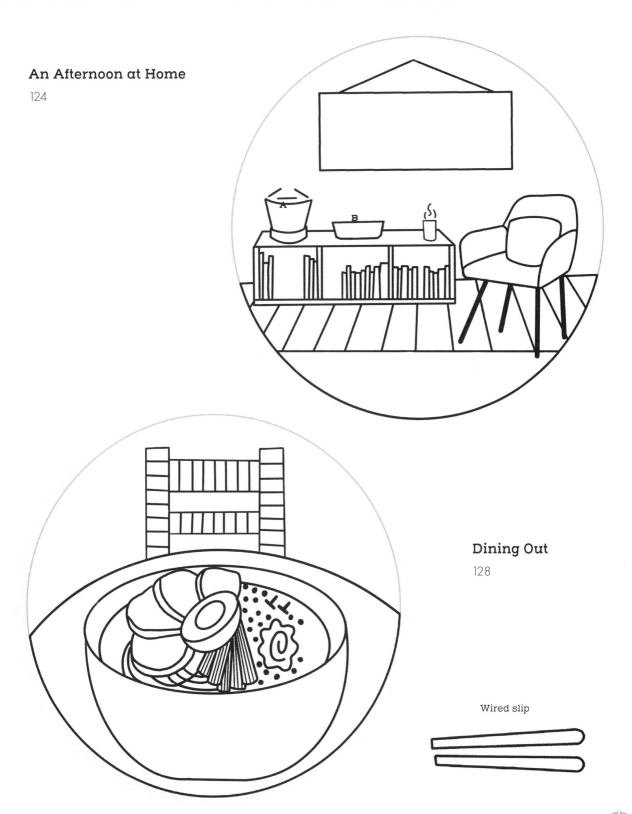

An Afternoon at Home

124

Dining Out

128

Wired slip

INDEX

Page numbers in **bold** type refer to templates.

YARNS USED

DMC colors

BLANC White

ECRU Off white

02 Tin oxide

17 Light yellow plum

20 Shrimp

23 Apple blossom

25 Ultra light lavender

29 Eggplant

32 Dark blueberry

35 Very dark fuchsia

167 Very dark yellow beige

168 Very light pewter

310 Black

351 Coral

355 Dark terra cotta

356 Medium terra cotta

367 Dark pistachio green

368 Light pistachio green

371 Mustard

400 Dark mahogany

420 Dark hazelnut brown

422 Light hazelnut brown

433 Medium brown

436 Tan

437 Light tan

500 Very dark blue green

502 Blue green

504 Very light blue green

522 Fern green

524 Very light fern green

543 Ultra very light beige

550 Very dark violet

561 Very dark jade green

730 Very dark olive green

738 Very light tan

758 Very light terra cotta

772 Very light yellow green

780 Ultra very dark topaz

819 Light baby pink

823 Dark navy blue

828 Ultra very light blue

830 Dark golden olive

890 Ultra dark pistachio green

894 Very light carnation

898 Very dark coffee brown

915 Dark plum

924 Very dark gray green

926 Medium gray green

935 Dark avocado green

936 Very dark avocado green

938 Ultra dark coffee brown

948 Very light peach

951 Light tawny

967 Very light apricot

976 Medium golden brown

3013 Light khaki green

3022 Medium brown gray

3031 Very dark mocha brown

3045 Dark yellow beige

3046 Medium yellow beige

3052 Medium green gray

3064 Desert sand

3348 Light yellow green

3371 Black brown

3771 Ultra very light terra cotta

3773 Medium desert sand

3777 Very dark terra cotta

3778 Light terra cotta

3810 Dark turquoise

3811 Very light turquoise

3820 Dark straw

3866 Ultra very light mocha brown

4501 Wildflowers coloris